D1636862

FARMERS MARKET COOKBOOK

BY FLORINE SIKKING
DESIGNED AND ILLUSTRATED BY GERRY ROSENTSWIEG
PUBLISHED BY ARMSTRONG PUBLISHING COMPANY
LOS ANGELES, CALIFORNIA

2

First Printing, July 1975

Copyright ©1975 by Armstrong Publishing Company
Library of Congress Catalog Card Number: 75-17329
Printed in the United States of America

ISBN 0—915936—01—1

Edited and Compiled By:
Jane Gilman and Dawne Goodwin,
the "Larchmont Chronicle"

Special thanks to our
home economist, Judith Zeidler

Thanks Also To:
Jean Armstrong
Ruth Caplan
Mary Duckworth
Josephine Goodwin
Betty Hansen
Barney Hartman
Alicja Kabacinski
Stephen J. Patrick
Suzanne Wallace

Published by:
Armstrong Publishing Company
5514 Wilshire Boulevard
Los Angeles, California 90036

Table of Contents

Preface

Whoever heard of "Barney Hartman's Mother's Green Tomato Pie?" Nobody, except for Barney Hartman, his mother, and maybe a few close and appreciative friends. But that's the whole idea here!

There are 151 more of these out-of-the-ordinary "family" recipes in this brand new one-of-a-kind souvenir remembrance called the "FARMERS MARKET COOKBOOK." Included are many of those most asked for by those who have come to the market over the years — now available all together for the first time.

Farmers Market at 3rd Street & Fairfax in Los Angeles is the marketplace par excellance, a friendly riot of colorful and wonderful things to oh and ah at, to eat and drink, to photograph, and to buy and take home to enjoy again.

Farmers Market has grown up gracefully with show business as its friend and neighbor. L.A. was emerging as the entertainment capital of the world when the market first opened for business in 1934. The shine has faded a little over the years, but movie-making studios still surround it — and right next door, a stone's throw away, is world-famous CBS Television City.

Today the Farmers Market is a combination of family-owned and operated "stalls" featuring locally grown produce and hand-created goods as well as internationally flavored foods, restaurants and wares. The original recipes in this book reflect the people of the market — some are traditional family recipes easy to prepare but with that "something special" added, while others are gourmet-inspired and adventurous to prepare and serve. Each of the 150 stalls of the market is represented in this book with its very own recipe. They're yours to read, remember and enjoy.

The Farmers Market Story

The Farmers Market is a continual festival of sights and sounds, and flavors, and smells, in the center of our nation's third largest city. Here, 150 individually owned and managed businesses — shops, stalls, stands, stores — cater to some 120,000 people weekly who walk through the Market's gates from every corner of the globe.

But back in 1934 the site of Farmers Market was only a dirt field, and the idea of the market was only a dream in the head of a Midwestern native named Roger Dahlhjelm.

Steak was then selling for 30¢ a pound, businessmen were going broke in the Great Depression, and Clark Gable was the young movie idol of millions of housewives.

A newly-completed state-wide water project began turning desert land in the San Fernando Valley into fertile fields, overflowing with fruits and produce. Newcomers to California were raving about "oranges big as grapefruit" and "mushrooms the size of silver dollars."

Dahlhjelm, financially reduced to bookkeeping in a Hollywood bakery, envisioned a marketplace where nearby farmers could sell their wares such as corn, melons, homemade jams, fresh eggs, country sausages, breads, cakes. He also wanted craftsmen to have a showcase to exhibit and sell their handmade products.

With the dream of a village of shops in the heart of Los Angeles, Dahlhjelm approached oilman Earl Gilmore. He asked Gilmore, who was a sports entrepreneur and large landowner as well, if he could lease land at Third and Fairfax for farmers and craftsmen.

The idea sounded good to Mr. Gilmore, although at that time he was more interested in the activities of the Pacific League football team, a baseball team, and midget auto racers at his Gilmore Stadium just north of the proposed market site.

The diligent Dahlhjelm convinced farmers in the San Fernando Valley to bring their very finest home-grown foods to his "Farmers Public Market."

On that first day, July 12, 1934, 18 trucks drove in from the San Fernando Valley and parked in the vacant lot to sell their vegetables, fruits, eggs, poultry. Twelve of the stalls were manned by farmers with produce and six other vendors offered foodstuffs such as sausages, cheeses, preserves, cakes and ice cream. Each vendor paid 50¢ per day to rent space on the market property.

It wasn't long before housewives began arriving in droves to buy the "better than anyone else's produce."

And Roger Dahlhjelm meticulously scrutinized the goods. He made sure the eggs were the freshest, the vegetables still damp from the morning soil, and the home-made goods the best available.

When he discovered that one vegetable man replenished his tomato supply from a nearby store instead of the fields, the vendor was promptly expelled. "We don't want cast-off foods," Dahlhjelm warned his prospective tenants. "If you try to pawn off yesterday's . parsnips, you'll be kicked out."

His strict standards paid off with success. Customers marveled over the myriad of quality foods which they could find nowhere else in the city.

In the following years the trucks were replaced with stands, stalls, and eventually roofs — a stick and a board at a time. The Market formed a Boys Band, hired an exclusive publicist, Fred Beck, and sponsored a radio show.

Farmers Market became a Los Angeles landmark, second only to Hollywood as a favorite place for tourists. By 1949 thousands of visitors were arriving daily, and the market was grossing $6 million annually.

Politicians, movie celebrities and professional athletes always made sure that their agenda while in Los Angeles included a stop at Farmers Market. And resident movie stars like Greta Garbo shopped here for edelweiss. Charlie Chaplin bought his kumquats here; other regulars over the years have been

Charles Laughton, Louella Parsons, Liberace, Ingrid Bergman, Danny Kaye, Paul Newman, President Dwight Eisenhower, Dinah Shore.

Although Roger Dahlhjelm died in 1949, he lived to see his dream of a Village become a reality. The food specialty shops multiplied and there were stores stocked with treasures from the world over, and restaurants offered the most delectable of menus.

To take over the reins of this marvelous market, Earl Gilmore named a young man fresh out of the Navy named John Gostovich. And it's been the spit-and-polish regime of Mr. Gostovich which has kept Farmers Market straight on course ever since.

John Gostovich
President
A. F. Gilmore Co.

The food area contains specialty meat, poultry and seafood shops; fruit and vegetable stalls, seven bakeries, a grocery, refreshment stands, and 27 kitchens and restaurants serving foods from Yankee pot roast to pizza, enchiladas to egg rolls, corned beef to barbecued chicken.

The Market has its own post office, travel bureau, car wash, barber shops, beauty shops, optometrist, art gallery. Every member of the family can be clothed, fed, cleaned, beautified, educated and entertained without ever leaving a Market gate.

There are also pet shops, a bank, bookshop, winery and plant nursery. But the ingredient that makes Farmers Market so marvelous is the people. The second and third generation of farmers and their families are now selling their prize-winning products to the great, the ordinary, the young, the old, the rich, the frugal, from all over the world. That's Farmers Market.

Tempting stalls feature never-ending supplies of vegetables, such as these avocados.

Founder of Farmers Market, Roger Dahlhjelm.

In the early years of the Farmers Market a boys band entertained customers during special promotions and parties.

Happiness is a convertible loaded with the finest in foods and groceries from Farmers Market.

APPETIZERS

"Bolsa Chica" Eggplant Appetizer

Here's how to take a basketful of Italian delicacies and turn them into a great hors d'oeuvre dish from Amalia's Handbags.

1/3 cup olive oil
1/3 cup red wine vinegar
pepper to taste
1 (or 2) 7½-oz can of caponata (found in most markets or in Italian delicatessens)
1 7-oz can solid light tuna packed in oil - rinsed and drained
14-oz can pimientos - drained and chopped
1 4-oz can green chili peppers
1 8½-oz can artichoke hearts - rinsed and drained

1 2-oz can anchovies - drained and chopped fine
1 5¾-oz can green olives
1 box fresh cherry tomatoes
1 16-oz can pearl onions - rinsed (fresh or frozen can be used — must be cooked)
1 15½-oz can garbanzo beans - rinsed
1 4-oz can sliced mushrooms — drained

Combine oil, vinegar and pepper. Combine all the remaining ingredients and toss well with the oil mixture. Chill several hours before serving. Makes 8-10 servings.

AMALIA'S HANDBAGS — Stall #140-G, H

Crab Mini-wiches

Dough experts at Clara and Joe's Bread Bin hope you'll enjoy these tasty appetizers.

1 7-oz can crab meat
2 hard cooked eggs, chopped
½ cup mayonnaise
¼ cup stuffed green olives, chopped
1½ tsp grated onion
8 slices bread (egg or sourdough)
½ cup butter
½ cup Parmesan cheese

Heat oven to 400°.
Combine first 5 ingredients. Butter one side of each piece of bread and spread with crab mixture to make sandwiches. Combine butter and cheese and spread outsides of sandwiches. Bake on cookie sheet for 10 minutes. Cut into eighths and serve. Makes 10-12 servings.

CLARA AND JOE'S BREAD BIN — Stall #330

Crabby Won Ton

George Chann, whose portraits and hand-painted works of art are famed, suggests this original creation.

1 4½-oz can crab meat (or ¼ lb fresh crab, shredded)
2 stalks celery, chopped very fine
½ medium onion, chopped very fine
3 tbs mayonnaise
½ tsp celery seed
½ tbs mayonnaise
salt and pepper
½ pkg won ton skins
vegetable oil
Parmesan cheese

Combine all ingredients except won ton skins, oil and Parmesan cheese and mix thoroughly. Fill each won ton skin with a scant teaspoon of mixture and fold into triangle, sealing edges with a few drops of water. In a large skillet, heat oil and fry filled won ton until golden brown, turning once. Drain on absorbent towel and sprinkle with Parmesan cheese while still hot.

GEORGE CHANN PORTRAITS — Stall #150

Spinach Leek Dip Supreme

Brighten your next cocktail party with custom-made crystal from Crystal Dreams, along with this sparkling spread.

1 pt sour cream
1 cup mayonnaise
¾ pkg dry leek soup mix
1 10-oz pkg frozen chopped spinach, thawed, well drained and re-chopped
½ cup fresh parsley, minced
½ cup green onions, minced
1 tsp dill weed
1 tsp salad seasoning mix
pinch of garlic powder
dash of nutmeg

Combine sour cream and mayonnaise. Add soup mix and combine thoroughly. Add remaining ingredients and mix well. Refrigerate overnight. Serve with thin slices of pumpernickel bread. Yield: 3½-4 cups dip.

CRYSTAL DREAMS — Stall #922

Opening Night Anchovy-Cheese Spread

Freshen up your collection of appetizer recipes with this spread from The Refresher.

1 8-oz pkg cream cheese
½ cup sweet butter
½ cup sour cream
½ tsp dry mustard
2 tsp capers, rinsed and chopped
2 tsp anchovy paste
¼ cup green onion, minced
2 tsp paprika
1 tbs caraway seeds
½ tsp salt

Combine all ingredients and beat until smooth, or mix with electric beater. Refrigerate several hours or overnight. Place spread in bowl and sprinkle top with additional ½ tsp caraway seeds. Serve with thin-sliced pumpernickel bread, party round bread or chips. Yield: 2½ cups dip.

THE REFRESHER — Stall #622

Tahineh
(sesame seed dip)

Buttons and Bows stocks buttons (and bows) from all over the world. Some of their loveliest are from Israel, setting of this unusual fare.

1 cup sesame seed paste	1 tsp salt
2 cloves garlic, crushed	juice of 2 lemons
½ cup water	dash cayenne pepper
	dash cumin

Combine all ingredients and blend into paste-like mixture. Add more water if necessary to work into paste. Serve in a bowl with pita bread on the side for dipping.
(Note: Should you wish to use this for a dressing, add water to make desired consistency.)

BUTTONS AND BOWS — Stall #150-12

Mrs. Gostovich's Boullion Dip

From the recipe file of Farmers Market general manager, John Gostovich, comes a superb compliment-catcher.

2 10½-oz cans bouillon	1 4-oz pkg cream cheese, room temperature
1½ pkgs gelatin	Worcestershire sauce
2 tbs bourbon	½ medium onion, pureed, or 1 tsp onion juice
3 drops Tabasco	2 tsp horseradish
1 tbs lemon juice	
dash of salt	
¼ tsp pepper	

Heat bouillon and add gelatin and completely dissolve. Add bourbon, tabasco, lemon juice, salt and pepper. Pour ½ bouillon mixture in mold to set. Blend together cream cheese, Worcestershire sauce, onion and horseradish. Pour cream cheese mixture over jellied bouillon mixture and add remaining bouillon mixture. Refrigerate for several hours. Unmold and serve with crackers. Makes 6-8 servings.

A. F. GILMORE COMPANY

Chipped Beef Dip a la "Beverly Hills"

The expert cobblers at Farmers Market Shoe Repair predict you'll get a lot of mileage from this tangy dip.

1 8-oz pkg cream
 cheese, softened
2 tbs milk
4¼ oz (1½ pkgs)
 dried beef
2 tbs onion, minced

2 tbs green pepper,
 minced
⅛ tsp pepper
½ cup sour cream
¼ cup walnuts,
 chopped

Heat oven to 350°.
Mix all of the above ingredients except nuts, in order, blending thoroughly before each addition. Place in a baking dish and sprinkle ¼ to ½ cup finely chopped walnuts over top. Bake 15 minutes; serve hot with sturdy crackers.

FARMERS MARKET SHOE REPAIR Stall #712

Crunchie Munchies "Cucamonga"

Dorothe-Maternity Fashions promises great expectations with these delicious morsels.

1 small pkg Cheerios
1 small pkg Corn
 Chex
1 pkg thin pretzel
 sticks
1 lb nuts (salted
 mixed or cashews)

¾ lb margarine,
 melted
¼ cup Worcester-
 shire sauce
2 tsp garlic salt
2 tsp onion salt
2 tsp celery salt

Heat oven to 250°.
In a large roasting pan, combine cheerios, corn chex, pretzels and nuts. Combine remaining ingredients and then pour over cereal mixture. Toss to mix. Bake for 2 hours, stirring every 20 minutes. To maintain crispness, store in sealed tins or plastic containers.

**DOROTHE-MATERNITY FASHIONS
Stall #150-33**

"Figueroa" Guacamole Dip

Famous California avocados are the main ingredient in this fabulous dip (or salad topping) from Fiesta Footwear.

**1 fresh tomato,
    peeled
2 avocados, peeled
    and pitted
½ onion, minced
1 tbs vinegar or
    lemon juice
½ tsp chili powder
salt and pepper to
    taste**

Mash tomato and avocado together until smooth. Add remaining ingredients and blend thoroughly. Cover tightly and chill at least 2 hours. Serve with taco chips, potato chips, or vegetables prepared for dipping.
(Note: raw carrots, celery, cauliflower, cherry tomatoes, jicama, cucumber and zucchini can be cut into strips and arranged on a platter. with guacamole in a dish in the center)

FIESTA FOOTWEAR — Stall #150-36

Empanadas

Castillo's Spanish Kitchen suggests this south of the border appetizer that's guaranteed to win applause.

1 lb ground meat
½ tsp cumin
½ tsp seasoned salt
½ cup green olives,
    pitted and sliced
½ cup black raisins
1 egg hard cooked,
    finely chopped
1 tube prepared
    crescent roll dough

Heat oven to 350°.
Salt a pan and stir-fry meat until crumbly and brown adding cumin while cooking. Combine salt, olives, raisins and egg and add to meat mixture. Cut the dough for each roll in half and fill with meat mixture, pinching ends to close. Bake on lightly greased cookie sheet for 15 minutes or until golden brown. Yield: 16 pieces

**CASTILLO'S SPANISH KITCHEN
Stall #322, 510**

"Wilshire Blvd." Walnut Cheese Ball

Impress your guests with this attractive appetizer from the cheese and sausage experts at the Hickory Farms of Ohio shop.

8 oz cream cheese,
    room temperature
3 oz bleu cheese,
    room temperature
4 oz cheddar cheese
    spread, room
    temperature
½ medium onion,
    grated
1½-2 cups walnuts,
    chopped
8-10 sprigs fresh
    parsley, chopped
    fine

Combine cheeses and mix thoroughly with electric mixer. Add onion and mix well. Shape into a ball and roll in chopped nuts and parsley that are evenly spread over plastic wrap. Refrigerate, wrapped in plastic wrap, overnight. Unwrap and serve with crackers.

HICKORY FARMS OF OHIO — Stall #116

Shanghai Shrimp Toast

Far East Traders, which imports beautiful wares from the Orient, offers this Far-Eastern appealing appetizer.

½ lb raw baby shrimp	1 tsp sugar
1 4-oz can water chestnuts, drained and chopped	1 tbs cornstarch
	1 egg, lightly beaten
2 scallions, chopped	6 slices bread (can be stale)
1 tsp salt	peanut oil

Mince shelled shrimp, mix with water chestnuts, scallions, salt, sugar, cornstarch and egg. Trim crusts off bread slices and spread each slice with shrimp mixture. Cut bread into 4 triangles. Heat oil to 375° in electric frypan, or on stove in skillet. Fry triangles until golden brown. Drain on paper towels. Makes 4-6 servings.

FAR EAST TRADERS — Stall #150-30

Party Time Crab Puffs

Polish up your culinary skills on this hot hors d'oeuvre from Shoe Shine and Plastic Lamination.

1 loaf white sandwich bread (day old is preferable)	1 7½-oz can crabmeat, chopped
8 oz cream cheese	1 cup parmesan cheese
6 tbs mayonnaise	2 egg whites, stiffly beaten
6 green onions with tops, chopped	5 or 6 drops Tabasco

Cut bread into 1¼" rounds. Cream together all ingredients in order, reserving ½ cup of parmesan cheese. Spread bread rounds with mixture. Dip each round in remaining cheese to seal. Place on cookie sheet and freeze. After frozen, can be stored in plastic bag. When ready to use, place frozen rounds on cookie sheet, heat under broiler until tops are golden. (Note: Should you wish to use without freezing, chill several hours then bake.)

**SHOE SHINE AND PLASTIC LAMINATION
Stall #752**

"La Brea Tar Pits" Marrow Bones

You'll rate compliments with gifts from Tunstall's Gift Shop and this unique dish.

**4 marrow bones,
    cut lengthwise in
    half (have butcher
    cut)**
**¼ lb margarine,
    unsalted**
**4 cloves garlic,
    crushed**
½ cup bread crumbs
1 tsp paprika
½ tsp salt

Heat oven to 400°.
Combine margarine and garlic and make into paste. Spread paste over the marrow side of bone. Sprinkle bread crumbs, paprika and salt on each bone. Place bones on cookie sheets and bake for 20 to 30 minutes until the marrow has turned creamy in color. Makes 8 servings.

TUNSTALL'S GIFT SHOP — Stall #150-6

Angels on Horseback

Scriptcraft Jewelry has forged a tasty sardine treat.

This is a typically English dish which is usually served for breakfast or brunch. It can be prepared the night before and kept in the refrigerator.

large sardines with skins
bacon, sliced
vegetable shortening, or bacon fat
white bread, sliced

Depending on how many people you serve, buy cans of large sardines (not skinless). Remove bacon from refrigerator so it will be at room temperature. Wrap each sardine in bacon, secure with toothpick. Place in skillet and brown, turning frequently. In second skillet, using either bacon fat, vegetable shortening or both, fry half slices of white bread until golden brown. Place on paper towels to drain in a warm oven. Put one sardine on each slice of bread and serve immediately.

SCRIPTCRAFT JEWELRY — Stall #140J

Artichokes "Los Angeles"

The sculpture at Kian's Gallery draws applause, and so will this artfully designed artichoke topped with green mayonnaise.

¼ cup mayonnaise
½ cup sour cream
2 tsp lemon juice
¼ tsp oregano, crushed
1 clove garlic, minced
¼ tsp Worcestershire sauce

¼ cup watercress leaves
¼ cup spinach leaves
¼ cup parsley sprigs
salt and pepper to taste
6 artichokes, cooked and chilled

Combine all ingredients except antichokes. Puree in electric blender until only small specks of green are visible. Salt and pepper to taste; cover and chill several hours. Arrange artichoke leaves on a platter, and place a small container of the dip in the center.

KIAN'S GALLERY — Stall #140-0

From teeny zucchini to giant tomatoes, the Market has them all.

SOUPS

"Mulholland Drive" Mushroom Potato Soup

Motorists and pedestrians alike will clean up with compliments with this recipe from Farmers Market Auto Wash.

½ lb fresh mushrooms or 1 3-oz can mushrooms	2 tbs butter, or margarine
1 cup potatoes, diced	2 tbs flour
¼ cup celery, chopped	2 cups milk
2 tbs onion, minced	1½ tsp salt
	½ tsp celery salt
	¼ tsp pepper
	1 tbs parsley, chopped

Slice mushrooms and set aside. Cook potatoes, celery and onion in water to cover, until tender. Do not drain. Melt butter in large pot, blend in flour and cook until lightly browned, stirring regularly. Add potato mixture, including liquid, and cook until smooth, stirring constantly. Stir in milk, mushrooms, salt, celery salt and pepper. Cook 10 to 15 minutes over low heat. Stir in parsley and serve. Makes 4-6 servings.

FARMERS MARKET AUTO WASH — Stall #120

Peanut Butter Soup!

Watch peanut butter being made at Magee's Nut Shop; then buy some to create this fantastic soup.

½ cup creamy
   peanut butter
3 cups chicken
   broth
1 cup half-and-half
½ tsp chili powder
½ tsp salt

Heat chicken broth (either homemade or canned — according to directions on can). When hot, place 1 cup of broth and the peanut butter in a blender; blend until smooth. Return to saucepan with remaining ingredients and bring to a boil; reduce heat to simmer and cook slowly for 15 minutes. Serve hot with a dab of whipped cream on top, or cold garnished with thin slices of cucumbers or radishes and whole peanuts. Makes 6 servings.

MAGEE'S NUT SHOP — Stall #218

Colossal Clam Chowder

Step into Oliver's Place and you'll think you are on New England shores, digging for clams to put into this Eastern favorite.

4 slices bacon, cut into small cubes
3 green onions and tops, chopped
5 medium potatoes, peeled and cut into ½ inch cubes
2 tbs green pepper, chopped
1 stalk celery, sliced
1 carrot, finely sliced
1 clove garlic, mashed
2 cups water
½ tsp pepper
1 tsp salt
1 tsp Worcestershire sauce
4 drops Tabasco
2 cups chopped clams with juice
1 8-oz can tomato sauce
1½ cups water (you may substitute part white wine for the water if you wish)

In a large, heavy kettle, saute bacon until crisp. Add onions, potatoes, green pepper, celery, carrot and garlic. Add water and seasonings and simmer 15 minutes or until potatoes are tender. Mash mixture slightly. If you prefer a thicker soup, mash well. In a separate pan, heat clams in their juice for 3 minutes. Add clams to potato mixture and pour in cream. Let stand for an hour or two. Reheat just until piping hot — do not boil. Makes 4 servings.

OLIVER'S PLACE — Stall #150-16

Spring Soup

Accentuate this Swedish-style Spring Soup with perky placemats and other table accessories from Roos Linens.

12 green onions (scallions), finely sliced
3 tbs butter or margarine
3 cups chicken broth (or 2 10½-oz cans)
3 carrots, peeled and julienned
4 stalks celery, julienned
1 cup half-and-half
1 cup milk
salt and pepper to taste
2 tbs fresh parsley, chopped

Saute half of the sliced scallions in butter until tender. Add more butter if necessary to avoid scorching of butter and scallions. Add chicken broth and bring to a simmer. Add carrots, celery and remaining scallions. When vegetables are tender, reduce heat and add half and half and milk, stirring constantly. Season with salt and pepper. Pour individual bowls and sprinkle with parsley. Makes 4 servings.

ROOS LINEN SHOP — Stall #150-4

Quick & Easy Lobster Bisque

Children's World knows mothers love time-saving ideas — like this good and quick and easy soup.

1 10½-oz can split
   pea soup
1 10½-oz can
   tomato soup
1 10½-oz can cream
   of mushroom
   soup
½ cup dry sherry
1 tsp salt
1 qt milk
½ lb lobster (or
   crab) meat
toasted sesame
   seeds

Blend together all the above ingredients except sesame seeds. Heat thoroughly at simmer. Sprinkle sesame seeds on top before serving. Makes 6 servings.

CHILDREN'S WORLD — Stall #150-14

Four-Star Lettuce Soup

Fresh produce is pampered at Vegetable Haven, like the ingredients for this lettuce soup.

1 head iceberg lettuce, rinsed, cored and drained	½ tsp salt
½ cup mayonnaise	½ tsp monosodium glutamate
2½ cups milk	½ tsp thyme
¼ cup butter or margarine	2 tbs sherry
3 tbs flour	¾ lb crab meat (fresh or canned)

Shred lettuce and combine with mayonnaise and 1 cup milk in blender and puree until smooth. Melt butter and add flour, salt, msg, thyme and cook until mixture is smooth and bubbling. Add remainder of milk and cook until thickened. Stir in pureed lettuce. Add sherry and crab meat, reserving 6 to 8 pieces for garnish. Heat soup but do not allow to boil. Serve in individual bowls and garnish with reserved crab meat. Makes 6-8 servings.

VEGETABLE HAVEN — Stall #122

Winter Melon Soup

From out of the pages of history comes this traditional Oriental specialty — as revealed by the Chinese Kitchen.

1 winter melon	1 8-oz can straw mushrooms
2 chicken breasts	
4 14½-oz cans clear chicken broth	1 4-oz can bamboo shoots, sliced or dice whole shoots into ½" pieces
pinch of white pepper	
salt to taste	
1 6-oz can water chestnuts, cut into fourths	1 12-oz can lotus nuts

Cut off top of melon and scoop out meat. Discard seeds and stringy fibers and dice melon into 1" cubes. Set aside shell of melon. Remove skin from chicken. Wash and dice chicken into ¾ to 1" pieces. Set aside. Bring chicken broth to boiling point. Add pinch of pepper, melon and chicken. Cover and simmer at medium heat for 20 minutes. Drain and rinse water chestnuts, straw mushrooms, bamboo shoots and lotus nuts. Add to chicken and melon the last 10 minutes of cooking. Salt to taste. Serve soup in melon shell. Makes 8-10 servings.

CHINESE KITCHEN
Stall #744

Curried Broccoli Soup

Rug Crafters popularity and yours, too, will increase when your guests taste their unusual soup.

2 lb broccoli (about
   2 bunches)
2 14 oz cans chicken
   broth
2 tbs butter
2 medium onions,
   chopped
2 tsp curry powder
sour cream
chopped salted
   peanuts

Trim off tough stems from broccoli and discard inedible portion. Cut off flowerets into bite-sized pieces. Coarsely chop stems and set aside. Bring 1 cup broth to boil in 3 quart pan. Add half of flowerets and cook uncovered 3-4 minutes until just tender when pierced with fork. Drain, save broth. Cool, cover and chill broccoli (to be used for garnish). In same pan, melt butter, add onions and curry powder. Cook until onions are translucent. Stir in broccoli stems, remaining flowerets and broth. Cover and simmer 12-15 minutes until tender when pierced. Whirl part of mixture at a time in blender until smooth. Cover and chill. Ladle into small bowls, top with chilled flowerets. Pass sour cream and peanuts. Makes 7 cups.

RUG CRAFTERS — Stall #150-16

Creamy Clam Chowder

There's nothing like home-made clam chowder and Ocean Foods has one of the best recipes for this tasty soup.

¼ lb salt pork, cut
   into ⅛-inch pieces
1 cup finely chopped
   onion
3 cups cold water
4 cups potatoes,
   peeled and cut into
   ¼" pieces
2 dozen shucked
   hard-shelled clams
   with their juice,
   coarsely chopped,
or two 8-oz cans
   chopped clams
   (about 2 cups)
2 cups heavy or
   light cream
⅛ tsp thyme
salt to taste
freshly ground
   pepper
2 tbs soft butter
paprika

Over high heat, fry the diced salt pork in a heavy 2-quart saucepan, stirring constantly for about 3 minutes until a thin film of fat covers the bottom of the pan. Reduce the heat to moderate, stir in the chopped onion and cook together for about 5 minutes longer, stirring occasionally. When the diced pork and onions turn a light golden brown, add 3 cups of water and the diced potatoes. Bring to a boil over high heat, then reduce the heat and simmer with the pan half covered for about 15 minutes until the potatoes are tender but not falling apart. Add the chopped clams and their juices, the cream and thyme, and heat almost to the boiling point. Then taste and season with salt and pepper. Stir in the soft butter. Serve in large individual bowls with each portion dusted with a little paprika. Makes 6-8 servings.

MICHAEL'S OCEAN FOODS — Stall #436

SALADS

Frozen Banana Salad

This whistle-winning recipe is "from the birds" — the flock at Coral Reef Bird Shop

1 tbs lemon juice
1 tsp salt
2 tbs mayonnaise
2 3-oz pkgs cream cheese
2 tbs crushed pineapple
1½ cups maraschino cherries, cut into quarters
½ cup walnuts, chopped
1 cup heavy cream, whipped
3 ripe bananas, cut into cubes
lettuce

Add lemon juice and salt to mayonnaise and stir into cream cheese. Add pineapple, cherries and nuts, fold in the whipped cream and then add bananas. Turn into refrigerator trays and place in freezer until firm. Remove, cut into squares and serve on crisp lettuce leaves with mayonnaise. Makes 8 servings.

CORAL REEF BIRD SHOP — Stall #1020

Grapefruit Boat Potpourri

Send your guests home shipshape with this pretty package of a salad from Wrap & Mail Service.

2 large grapefruit
8 oz tiny bay shrimp
1 banana, sliced
juice of ½ a lemon
1 cucumber, peeled and diced
4 slices canned pineapple, diced and drained
1 tbs mustard
3 tbs ketchup
dash of pepper
¼ tsp paprika
1 tbs fresh horse-radish, grated (or 2 tbs prepared horseradish)
1 8-oz carton yogurt, plain
½ cup heavy cream, whipped

Cut grapefruit in half and remove seeds. Cut around inside edge as close to skin shell as possible. Separate grapefruit segments from membrane. Chill grapefruit shells (optional). Discard membrane and dice segments. Combine grapefruit, shrimp, and banana with lemon juice. Add cucumber and pineapple. Mix well and cover with foil and chill several hours. Mix together mustard, ketchup, pepper, paprika, horseradish and yogurt. Fold in cream. Remove fruit with slotted spoon and fill chilled grapefruit shells or chilled bowls with mixture. Top with dressing. Makes 4 servings.

WRAP AND MAIL SERVICE — Stall #150-37

"Grauman's Chinese" Food Salad

Du-Par's Restaurant is famous for originating delicious foods here in Los Angeles. But they really traveled far afield for this salad.

Dressing:
1 cup vegetable oil
¼ cup white vinegar, or cider vinegar
1/3 cup ketchup
2/3 cup sugar
1 medium onion, grated
salt and pepper

Combine all ingredients and mix well. Let stand while preparing salad.

Salad:
1 lb fresh spinach, washed, dried and torn in bite-size pieces
1 lb fresh bean sprouts, washed and dried
1 5-oz can water chestnuts, sliced thin
¼ lb fresh mushrooms, sliced

Combine all salad ingredients in large bowl. Pour over half of dressing mixture, and toss. Each piece of salad should be well coated. Add more dressing if desired. Makes 4 servings.

DU-PAR'S RESTAURANT — Stall #210

Caesar Salad Tijuana

A true California speciality that appeals to hearty appetites from those connoisseurs of men's styles of Campbell's Men's Shop.

3 cloves garlic, chopped
1½ cups olive oil
3 quarts salad greens, washed and torn in bite-size pieces
¼ cup Parmesan cheese, grated
¼ cup bleu cheese, or Roquefort
1 tbs Worcestershire sauce
½ tsp dry mustard
salt and pepper
1 egg, beaten
½ cup fresh lemon juice
2 cups croutons

Soak garlic in one cup of oil for several hours at room temperature. Put salad greens in a large bowl and coat with remaining ½ cup oil, Parmesan cheese and blue cheese. Toss well. Add Worcestershire sauce, mustard, salt and pepper. Toss well. Pour egg and lemon juice over greens and toss again, making sure that every leaf is coated with egg, seasoning and cheese. Dip croutons into garlic-flavored oil and add to salad. Serve at once. Makes 6-8 servings.

CAMPBELL'S MEN'S SHOP — Stall #150-32

Corned Beef Salad "Chula Vista"

Far-sighted chefs know they can prepare Trask Optician salad days ahead.

1½ tbs unflavored gelatin
1/3 cup cold water
2 bouillon cubes
2 cups boiling water
½ tsp Worcestershire sauce
½ tsp salt
1 cup diced celery
¾ cup canned peas, drained
½ cup sliced radishes
½ cup diced pickled beets
6 oz pressed corn beef, pulled in pieces

Dissolve gelatin in the 1/3 cup cold water. Dissolve the bouillon cubes in the 2 cups boiling water and pour over gelatin. Stir until mixed. Add Worcestershire sauce and salt. Chill. When the mixture begins to thicken, add the remaining ingredients. Pour the mixture in molds of any shape desired. Refrigerate several hours. When thoroughly chilled, turn out on crisp lettuce leaves, garnish with cucumber pickles and serve with mayonnaise dressing. This is an excellent Sunday night supper dish. Makes 4 servings.

**KENNETH TRASK, OPTICIANS
Stall #150-7**

Seaside Rainbow Salad

The thoughtful staff at Farmers Market Stationery 'N Cards says this salad is a cheerful addition to the meal.

½ lb frozen, de-veined shrimp
1 cup frozen blueberries, defrosted and drained
¼ cup green pepper, diced
¼ cup red pepper, diced
1 firm tomato, sliced
3 radishes, thinly sliced
½ cup celery, diced
½ cup cucumber, sliced
½ head lettuce, broken into bite-size pieces
thousand island dressing

Defrost shrimp under cold water. Combine all ingredients in a large, chilled salad bowl and serve with Thousand Island Dressing. Makes 4 servings.

**FARMERS MARKET STATIONERY
'N CARDS — Stall #150-26**

"Alvarado" Avocado

A zesty shrimp salad nested in avocado is courtesy of the menu collection at Loretta's Needlepoint.

¼ **cup tarragon vinegar**
2 **tbs horseradish mustard**
1 **tbs ketchup**
1½ **tsp paprika**
½ **tsp salt**
¼ **tsp cayenne pepper**

½ **cup salad oil**
¼ **cup celery, minced**
¼ **cup green onions, minced with tops**
2 **lbs shrimp, cooked and cleaned**
4 **medium avocados**

In a small bowl combine vinegar, mustard, ketchup, paprika, salt and pepper. Slowly add oil, beating constantly. Stir in celery and onions. Pour sauce over shrimp and chill 4-5 hours. Peel and halve avocados. Lift shrimp out of sauce and arrange 5 or 6 in each avocado half. Serve with remaining sauce. Makes 8 servings.

LORETTA'S NEEDLEPOINT STUDIO
Stall #150-9

Nebraska Shrimp Salad

This recipe is taken from the pages of Time-Life Books.

1 can tomato soup
2 3-oz pkg cream cheese
2 3-oz pkg lemon gelatin
1 1/3 cups hot water
1½ cups chopped celery
2 tbs grated onion
½ cup finely chopped red pepper, or ¼ cup chopped pimiento
1 cup chopped nuts
1 cup Miracle Whip salad dressing, or ½ cup sour cream mixed with ½ cup salad dressing
1 cup very small shrimp

Heat tomato soup, melt cream cheese in it. Beat until smooth and cool. Dissolve gelatin in hot water and cool to heavy syrup stage. Add to cheese mixture and add salad dressing and all other ingredients. Pour into individual molds or one large mold that will serve 12. Chill. Makes 12 servings. From "Great Dinners from Life" Cookbook.

TIME LIFE BOOKS, INC. — Stall #140-F

Mrs. Wiggs Cabbage Mold

Solve your gift problems with a visit to the Gift Nook — and add this colorful salad to your kitchen repertoire.

2 3-oz pkgs lime gelatin
1 cup boiling water
1 cup cold water
4 tbs white or apple cider vinegar
1 cup mayonnaise
½ tsp salt
dash pepper
4 cups cabbage, grated fine
2 tbs onion, chopped fine
1 tsp celery seed

Dissolve gelatin in hot water, then add cold water. Add vinegar, mayonnaise, salt and pepper and mix well. Chill until thick for about 3-4 hours. Beat gelatin mixture with beater and add cabbage, onion and celery seed. Pour into mold and chill until firm. Makes 6 servings.

GIFTS AND GADGET NOOK
Stalls #112, 228, 528

Cranberry Nugget Mold

Here's a gem of a recipe from Farmers Market Gem Shop to brighten your next dining occasion.

1 3-oz pkg
  strawberry gelatin
1 cup boiling water
1 cup jellied cran-
  berry sauce
1 cup apples,
  chopped

1 cup celery,
  chopped
1 cup walnuts,
  chopped

Dissolve gelatin in boiling water, add cranberry sauce. Whip to cool and dissolve. Fold in apples, celery and walnuts. Chill until firm in 3 to 4 cup mold — serve on lettuce garnished with cut fresh fruit or strawberries. Makes 6 servings.

**FARMERS MARKET GEM SHOP
Stall #150-27**

Raspberry Refresher

Fashions from Lorraine Kaye's are as yummy as this recipe that will do for either salads or dessert.

**1 10-oz pkg frozen
    raspberries
1 3-oz pkg raspberry
    gelatin
½ cup boiling water
¾ cup dry sherry
¼ cup lemon juice
½ pt heavy cream
1 tbs powdered
    sugar
3 drops vanilla**

Defrost raspberries and reserve juice. Dissolve gelatin in hot water and stir until clear. Add sherry, lemon juice and juice from raspberries. Stir in raspberries and place in mold or parfait glasses. Refrigerate several hours. Whip cream until stiff. Add sugar and vanilla and mix well. Top each serving with a spoonful of whipping cream. Makes 4 servings.

LORRAINE KAYE FASHIONS — Stall #150-16

Millionaires Kumquat Salad

Invest in kumquats to create this dividend of a salad from Gilmore Commercial and Savings Bank, a full-service financial institution.

**1 3-oz pkg lemon
    gelatin
½ cup boiling water
1¼ cup ginger ale
¼ cup kumquat
    juice (reserved from
    canned kumquats)**

**¼ tsp salt
1¼ cups canned
    kumquats, drained
    and sliced
1 avocado, peeled
    and sliced**

Dissolve gelatin in hot water. Add ginger ale and kumquat juice and mix thoroughly. Add remaining ingredients and pour into a mold. Chill for several hours. Unmold and serve. Makes 4-6 servings.

**GILMORE COMMERCIAL
AND SAVINGS BANK**

Juicy Tropical Salad

Boris Juice and Salad Bar furnish a dish inspired by their orchard of fruit drinks — everything from apricot to mango. Try the "Yummy Yogurt Dressing" too.

1 head iceberg or
   butter lettuce,
   washed
2 grapefruit, peeled
   and sectioned
2 oranges, peeled
   and sectioned
2 papayas, peeled
   and wedged

2 avocados, peeled
   and wedged
¼ fresh pineapple,
   peeled and
   chunked
6 maraschino
   cherries

Place a lettuce leaf on each salad plate and arrange alternately grapefruit, orange and papaya. In the center, place avocado and pineapple. Garnish with cherries. Serve with Yogurt Dressing. Makes 4-6 servings.

Yogurt Dressing

1 cup yogurt
2 tbs mayonnaise
1 tsp white
   granulated sugar,
   or brown sugar

¼ tsp lemon juice
pinch of salt

Combine all ingredients, mixing thoroughly. Chill well. Serve over fresh fruit of the season. Yield - About 1 cup

BORIS JUICE AND SALAD BAR — Stall #334

Angeleno Ambrosia

The Brush Shop solves your cleaning problems with its 1000's of brushes. You'll clean up the compliments with this dessert.

1 pt sour cream
2 cups pineapple
   tidbits
1½ cups marsh-
   mallow tidbits
1½ cups flaked
   coconut

Place sour cream in large mixing bowl and whip until quite thin. Mix drained pineapple, marshmallows and coconut into whipped sour cream. Blend well. Mixture should look a little thin, but this allows the marshmallows and coconut to absorb the pineapple and sour cream. Cover with plastic wrap, refrigerate at least overnight, preferably 24 hours.
May be used as a fruit salad or a dessert. Very good with turkey or ham dinners, and an excellent addition to almost any buffet. May be varied by adding sliced fresh orange sections chunked and/or chopped almonds. Keeps several days. Serving suggestion: Cut orange in half and hollow out fruit. Fill shells with ambrosia. Makes 8-10 servings.

BRUSH SHOP — Stall #152

California Spiced Orange Wedges

Bisbano's Citrus stall is brimming with big beautiful oranges like the ones you'll want to use for this perky salad.

**4 Valencia oranges,
   unpeeled
2 cups sugar
1 1/3 cups water
½ cup cider vinegar
12 whole cloves
3 pieces cinnamon
   bark**

Add enough water in a saucepan to cover oranges and bring to a boil. Cook about 20 minutes or until easily pierced with a knife. Remove oranges with slotted spoon and cut into eighths. Combine remaining ingredients in saucepan and stir over low heat until sugar is dissolved. Bring to a boil and add orange slices. Lower heat and simmer for 20 minutes. Cool and store, covered, in refrigerator. Serve with beef or lamb dishes.

BISBANO'S CITRUS — Stall #126

"El Rey" Green Goddess Dressing

This heavenly dressing is from King's Casuals, which features sportswear for both goddesses and mere earthlings.

**1 pt sour cream
1 tbs mayonnaise
1 tbs wine vinegar
4 green onions,
   chopped fine
¼ tube anchovy
   paste
½ bunch parsley,
   chopped very fine
dash pepper
salt (optional)**

Combine all ingredients and blend thoroughly. Chill several hours to enhance flavor. Serve over Romaine lettuce. (Can garnish with sliced anchovies.) Yield: 1 pt dressing.

KING'S CASUALS — Stall #150-35

Russian Dressing "Extra"

Keep up-to-date on world affairs at Farmers Market Newsstand; keep salads international with this dressing.

1 10½-oz can
tomato soup
1 cup oil
¾ cup vinegar
½ cup sugar
2 tsp salt
1 tsp paprika
1 tbs dry mustard
1 tbs onion, grated
2 tbs Worcestershire
sauce

Combine tomato soup, oil and vinegar and beat well. Mix together sugar, salt, paprika and dry mustard and add to tomato mixture. Add onion and Worcestershire sauce and mix thoroughly. Store, covered, in refrigerator.
(Note: One-eighth lb crumbled Roquefort cheese can be added to this recipe for a delicious variation.) Yield: 3 cups.

FARMERS MARKET NEWSSTAND
Stall #550

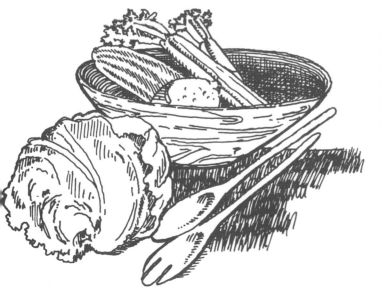

Sun-shiney French Dressing

Bryan's Pit Barbecue suggest you accompany those charcoal-flavored steaks (from their place or yours) with a salad mixed with their special French Dressing.

1 cup ketchup
¼ cup granulated
**   sugar**
½ tsp salt
½ tsp dry mustard
¼ tsp paprika
1 medium clove
**   garlic, crushed**
1 cup lemon juice
1 cup mayonnaise

Mix thoroughly all ingredients, or place in blender and blend for 2 minutes. Chill overnight to improve flavor. Yield: 3 cups

Sky-bleu Cheese Dressing

Or try this West Coast favorite, furnished by Bryan's Pit Barbecue.

1 cup buttermilk
6 oz bleu cheese,
**   crumbled**
1 small clove garlic,
**   crushed**
6 green onions,
**   chopped fine**
½ tsp salt
1 cup mayonnaise

Combine all ingredients except mayonnaise in blender, or mix by hand until cheese and vegetables are fine. Add mayonnaise and mix just until smooth. Chill overnight to blend flavors. Yield: 2½ cups

BRYAN'S PIT BARBECUE — Stall #740

VEGETABLES

Nutty Creamed Onions

Here's a memento from the Redwood Shop, which sell fine souvenirs of California's stately trees.

16 whole small white onions
2 tbs butter or margarine
2 tbs flour
¼ tsp salt
2 cups milk

½ cup whole shelled salted peanuts
½ cup buttered bread crumbs
¼ cup salted peanuts, coarsely chopped

Heat oven to 400°.
Grease 1-quart casserole.
Cook onions in boiling salted water until tender, drain. Melt butter over medium heat, stir in flour and salt. Remove from heat and slowly add milk and blend. Return to heat and cook until thickened, stirring constantly. Place onions in casserole and cover with butter and milk mixture. Stir in ¼ cup whole peanuts. Top with crumbs and chopped peanuts.
Bake for 15 minutes or until bubbly and lightly browned. Makes 4 servings.

REDWOOD SHOP — Stall #150

West Coast Baked Beans

Accompany a meal of fine Tusquellas Meat with this exclusive family recipe.

1 lb pink beans, soaked overnight
1 tsp salt
1 medium onion, chopped
1 12-oz bottle chili sauce
2 tbs dark molasses
2 tbs brown sugar
1 tsp mustard (prepared)
½ lb bacon, sliced

Add salt to soaked beans and boil for 4 hours.
Heat oven to 325°.
Put beans in 3 qt casserole; pour in enough of the water the beans were cooked in to cover. Add remaining ingredients, topping the mixture with the bacon slices. Bake, covered, for 5 hours. (If pyrex casserole is used, reduce temperature to 300° for 5 hours.) Makes 6-8 servings.

TUSQUELLAS MEAT — Stall #350

Ratatouille

Bruce William's Western Frontier #2 bring you this mouth-watering recipe for Ratatoulle.

- 3 cloves garlic, chopped
- 1 medium onion, chopped
- ½ to ¾ cup olive oil
- 2 zucchini, sliced thick
- 1 green pepper, chunked
- 1 eggplant, peeled and chunked
- 3 tomatoes, peeled & quartered
- salt and pepper to taste

Saute garlic and onion in oil and remove with slotted spoon when slightly golden and set aside. Saute each vegetable in the oil until just tender and then remove with slotted spoon, zucchini, green pepper, eggplant and tomatoes. The eggplant tends to absorb the oil so additional oil may be needed. Return all ingredients to pan to reheat, add salt and pepper to taste and serve immediately. Makes 4 to 6 servings.

BRUCE WILLIAM'S WESTERN FRONTIER #2
Stall #140-E

Silver Screen Eggplant Souffle

Only Meshulam's Fruit Fair could have the expertise to contribute this unique eggplant dish.

- 2 large broiled or steamed eggplants, peeled
- 4 tbs butter or margarine
- 1 medium onion, chopped
- 1¼ cups grated Romano cheese or Parmesan cheese
- ½ cup bread crumbs
- 5 eggs, beaten

Place eggplants on pan under broiler until skin appears to be shriveling. Turn gradually, until all sides are cooked. (Should you prefer to steam the eggplants, peel and cut in large chunks and place in saucepan with minimal amount of water. Cover and cook until tender, about 10 minutes. Remove eggplant and press out any excess liquid.)
Heat oven to 350°.
Chop or mash eggplant and set aside. Saute onion in butter until clear and tender. Add to eggplant and then add cheese (reserving 2 tbs for top), bread crumbs and eggs, mixing thoroughly. Pour mixture in a well greased souffle dish and top with cheese. Bake for 45 minutes. Makes 8-10 servings.

MESHULAM'S FRUIT FAIR — Stall #424

"Burbank" Cauliflower Patties

One of the original stalls is Meshulam's Burbank Stall. They pass along a novel vegetable dish using some of their fabulous produce.

**1 medium cauli-
flower, boiled and
chopped
1 onion, finely
chopped
¼ cup parsley, finely
chopped
½ cup bread crumbs
3 eggs, beaten
½ tsp salt
½ cup flour
vegetable oil**

Combine cauliflower, onion, parsley, bread crumbs, 2 eggs and salt and mix thoroughly. Shape into 4" patties and dip in remaining egg and flour. Heat oil and fry each patty until golden brown. Drain on absorbent paper. Makes 4 servings.

**MESHULAM'S BURBANK STALL
Stall #518**

Barney Hartman's Mother's Green Tomato Pie

Barney Hartman, right-hand-man to A.F. Gilmore Co. president John Gostovich, convinced his mother to share this family-only recipe.

2 cups green
   tomatoes, peeled
   and sliced
1 cup brown sugar
1 tbs flour
1 tbs vinegar
½ tsp cinnamon
⅛ tsp nutmeg

½ tsp salt
4 tbs butter or
   margarine
2 tbs granulated
   sugar
pastry for 2 crust
   pie

Heat oven to 425°.
Combine all ingredients except 2 tbs butter and granulated sugar in a bowl and mix thoroughly. Line an 8" pie shell with pastry. Fill with tomato mixture. Seal top with second pastry and press edges together. Dot top of crust with remaining butter and sprinkle with granulated sugar. Bake at 425° for 10 minutes; reduce heat to 375° and bake 40 minutes.

A.F. GILMORE COMPANY

Vegetables Fantastique

Trust Kludjian's Farm Fresh Produce to create a culinary masterpiece using a variety of their flavorful vegetables.

3 green peppers
3 firm tomatoes
3 medium zucchini
3 summer squash
1½ lbs ground beef
   or lamb shoulder
½ cup rice, raw
3 medium onions,
   chopped fine

3 tbs parsley,
   chopped fine
salt and pepper
½ cup water
1 15-oz can tomato
   sauce

Prepare vegetables for stuffing:
Cut top off peppers and tomatoes and remove pulp. Set aside tomato pulp for stuffing. Cut zucchini lengthwise in half and remove pulp. Cut stem and top off summer squash and carefully remove pulp.
Prepare stuffing:
Heat oven to 350°.
Knead the meat with tomato pulp, rice, onion, parsley, salt and pepper. Fill the hollows of the vegetables with meat mixture and arrange side by side in a baking pan. Combine water and tomato sauce and pour equal amount on each vegetable. Cover with aluminum foil and bake 1½ hours. Makes 4-6 servings.

**KLUDJIAN'S FARM FRESH PRODUCE
Stall #816**

"Movieland" Marshmallow Yams

Coral Reef Gift Shop recommends an out-of-the-ordinary side dish with marshmallow "frosting."

8 medium size yams
1 tbs butter or
    margarine
½ cup hot milk
salt
1 tsp cinnamon
1 tsp nutmeg
¼ tsp paprika
1 cup walnuts,
    chopped in
    medium-sized
    pieces
½ lb marshmallows

Bake or boil yams in their jackets until tender. Cool, peel and mash. Add all ingredients except marshmallows and mix thoroughly. Place in buttered baking dish. Cover top with marshmallows. Heat in 350° oven until marshmallows are golden brown. Makes 12-16 servings.

CORAL REEF GIFT SHOP — Stall #920

Hot Curried Fruit

The Paper Shop provides party accessories for every occasion, including the special one when you serve this spicy side dish.

1 16-oz can pear
    slices, drained
    (reserve juice)
1 16-oz can apricot
    halves, drained
    (reserve juice)
1 14-oz can pine-
    apple chunks,
    drained, (reserve
    juice)
1 8-oz jar maraschino
    cherries, drained

2 tbs butter, room
    temperature
2 tbs dark brown
    sugar
1 tsp curry powder
2 tsp cornstarch
½ tsp grated lemon
    peel
½ cup cream sherry

Combine all fruit in a 1½-quart casserole. Mix lightly to avoid breaking fruit. Combine remaining ingredients in separate bowl and mix well. Sprinkle over fruit and let stand several hours. Heat oven to 325°.
Before baking, add ¼ cup of the combined reserved juices. Bake uncovered for one hour. Spoon juices over fruit every 15 minutes while baking. Makes 6 servings.

PAPER SHOP — Stalls #150-D and 150-5

Tasty Zucchini Casserole

Accompany this casserole with one of Barengo Winery's fabulous assortment of wines and liqueurs from California vineyards.

1 medium onion, thinly sliced	dash garlic powder
3 tbs olive or salad oil	dash monosodium glutamate
1 lb ground beef	1 tbs sugar
3 8-oz cans tomato sauce	salt and pepper to taste
1 cup Burgundy wine	2 lbs zucchini (6 or 7 medium size)
1 tsp Italian style seasoning	grated Parmesan cheese

Heat oven to 350°.
Using a large skillet or Dutch oven, saute onion in butter until clear. Add beef, stir regularly until browned. Add tomato sauce, wine and seasoning. Cover, simmer gently for 1 hour, stirring occasionally. Wash and cut ends off zucchini and boil whole in salted water for 12 minutes, or until just tender. Drain. When cool enough to handle, cut in half lengthwise. Place, cut side up, in greased shallow baking pan. Pour sauce over zucchini and bake for 45 minutes. Sprinkle grated Parmesan cheese on top. Makes 4-6 servings.

BARENGO WINERY

Gingered Cucumber Jewels

Strike it rich with this bonanza of gingered cucumbers from Gold Mine Jewelers, which imports 14 and 18 karat gold jewelry.

1 tbs salt
3 cucumbers, peeled and thinly sliced
½ cup cider or white vinegar
5 tbs sugar
1 tbs fresh ginger, grated
1 tsp sesame seeds, toasted

Sprinkle salt on cucumbers and let stand 5-10 minutes. Combine all remaining ingredients in a saucepan and bring to a boil. While still hot, pour vinegar mixture over cucumbers and mix well. Refrigerate, covered, until ready to serve.

GOLD MINE JEWELERS — Stall #156½

Senor Cole Porter's Welsh Rarebit

Little Mexico Mart's friendship with Cole Porter resulted in a gourmet recipe from the files of this famed composer.

1 tsp Hungarian
  paprika
1/8 tsp salt
dash black pepper,
  finely ground
1½ tsp Worcester-
  shire sauce
1/16 tsp Tabasco
1 egg, beaten

1½ lbs medium
  Tillamook cheese,
  cubed in small
  pieces
1 28-oz can
  tomatoes, drained
2 to 3 oz beer
2 pkgs Uneeda
  unsalted biscuits,
  buttered
Major Grey's Indian
  Mango Chutney

In a small mixing bowl, place paprika, salt and pepper. Stir in Worcestershire sauce and tabasco, making a smooth paste. Add egg and mix until smooth. In a double boiler, place cheese and stir constantly until melted. Add tomatoes, stirring and mashing them until texture is even and bubbling. Gradually add eggs and Worcestershire sauce mixture and mix until thoroughly heated. Add beer and allow to foam on top and then stir until heated. Additional beer may be added if texture is not consistency of soft whipped cream. Spoon mixture over crackers and arrange in groups of four on individual dishes. Top with ½ tsp of chutney. Makes 4 servings.

LITTLE MEXICO MART — Stall #150-29

Stuffed Mushrooms "Bel Air"

What the fruit and vegetable stands don't have, Alexander's Grocery does. Delight your dinner guests with this Alexander exclusive.

½ cup butter, or margarine
1/3 cup shallots, chopped (or freeze dried)
3 tbs chives, chopped (or freeze dried)
1 tbs parsley, chopped

white wine
18 whole fresh mushroom caps
1 cup mushroom pieces and stems, chopped
Mushroom-Base Sauce
¾ cup roasted almonds, chopped

Melt butter in saucepan and add 1/3 of the shallots, chives and parsley. Add enough wine to cover ingredients. Add mushrooms caps and saute until they start to soften. Remove caps from liquid and set aside in greased oven-proof dish. Add chopped mushrooms to liquid, adding more wine if necessary. Strain liquid into Mushroom-Base Sauce and place remaining cooked mushrooms, chives, shallots and parsley in a bowl. Add all remaining shallots, chives, parsley and almonds. Mix well. Add one tablespoon at a time of Mushroom Sauce until mixture holds together. Stuff caps with stuffing mixture, heaping high. Top with Mushroom Sauce and place under broiler until bubbling hot. Makes 8-10 servings.

MUSHROOM-BASE SAUCE

½ cup butter, or margarine
3 tbs shallots, chopped
3 tbs chives, chopped
1 tbs parsley, chopped
1 cup white wine

1 cup fresh mushrooms, chopped
1½ cups water
1 tbs strong chicken stock
1 tbs strong beef stock
½ cup red wine
3 tbs cornstarch

Melt butter in saucepan and add shallots, chives, parsley and ¼ cup white wine and cook for 2 minutes. Add mushrooms and enough additional white wine to cook them. Cook 3-5 minutes. Add water, chicken and beef stock, red wine and bring to a boil. Dissolve cornstarch in ¼ cup white wine and gradually add to mixture, stirring constantly until all ingredients are thoroughly blended. Makes 2 cups sauce.

ALEXANDER'S GROCERY — Stall #150

Eggplant Casserole Italiano

Eggplant is only one of the gorgeous vegetables available from Bisbano's Produce. They cook it a very special way.

2 cloves garlic, chopped
1 onion, chopped
olive oil
2 lbs tomatoes, peeled and chopped or 2 16-oz cans whole tomatoes
2 cups water
1 tbs sweet basil
1 bay leaf

salt and pepper to taste
1 eggplant, peeled and sliced about ½"-¾" thick
2 green peppers, sliced
grated Romano cheese
1 lb zucchini, sliced

Sauce:
Saute garlic and onion in olive oil. Add tomatoes and 2 cups water. Bring to a boil. Add sweet basil, bay leaf, salt and pepper. Cook on low heat until sauce begins to thicken. Remove from heat.

To assemble casserole:
Heat oven to 350°.
Put a layer of sauce in bottom of 1½-quart casserole. Layer with eggplant, grated cheese, sauce, green pepper, zucchini, sauce, and repeat, beginning with eggplant, until all ingredients are used, ending with sauce and cheese on top. Casserole can be assembled to this point and refrigerated, or frozen, until ready to bake. Bring to room temperature and bake one hour. Makes 4 servings.

BISBANO'S PRODUCE — Stall #130

Gnocchi Verde

This recipe from Patsy's Pizza is as Italian as a stroll down the Via Veneto.

**10 oz fresh spinach
   leaves, washed
1 lb ricotta cheese
1 egg
½ tsp nutmeg
salt
4 tsp Parmesan
   cheese, grated
¼ cup flour
butter (unsalted)**

Cook spinach in salted water, drain. Chop fine and mix with ricotta cheese. Add egg, nutmeg and dash of salt and mix well. Add Parmesan cheese. Add flour and blend until mixture is smooth. Take ½ tbs of mixture and roll in flour. Bring 4 quarts of water to a boil and add 5 tsp salt. Drop gnocchi in water one at a time, just filling bottom of pot. When they rise to top they are done. Remove with slotted spoon. Butter large serving tray and fill with gnocchi and sprinkle with Parmesan cheese. Makes 6 servings.

PATSY'S PIZZA — Stall #448

Fairfax Lukshen Kugel

When Phil's Roundup sounds the dinner gong, be sure to include this noodle pudding.

**½ lb wide noodles
3 tbs butter or
   margarine, melted
3 egg yolks
2 tsp cinnamon
½ tsp vanilla
1 cup sugar
2 cooking apples,
   peeled and sliced**

**½ cup white raisins,
   washed
1 cup cottage
   cheese
3 egg whites, stiffly
   beaten
1 pt sour cream**

Heat oven to 350°.
In a large saucepan, cover noodles with boiling water and cook until just tender. Drain noodles and return to large saucepan. Pour butter over noodles, stirring constantly with wooden spoon until noodles are coated and no butter remains in bottom of pan. Remove from heat. In a bowl, beat egg yolks and add to them cinnamon, vanilla, sugar, apples, raisins and cottage cheese. Add egg mixture to noodles. Fold in stiffly beaten egg whites. Pour into a well-greased baking dish and bake 45 minutes or until brown on top. Serve hot, topped with sour cream. Makes 6-8 sevings.

PHIL'S ROUNDUP — Stall #540

This windmill was the original symbol of Farmers Market.

BREADS

Discs of Pita Bread

At Farmers Market Records & Radio they sing the praises of this harmonious treat.

½ cup warm water
2 pkgs yeast
¼ tsp granulated
  sugar
2 cups warm water

3 tbs olive oil
1½ tsp salt
6 cups flour
¼ cup vegetable oil

Combine water, yeast and sugar and stir until yeast is dissolved. Set aside. In a mixing bowl combine water, olive oil and salt. Add yeast mixture to mixing bowl and blend thoroughly. Sift in flour, one cup at a time, blending thoroughly between additions. Turn dough out onto a floured board and knead about 10-12 minutes. Oil a large bowl and put in dough. Oil top of dough lightly with vegetable oil. Cover with a towel and let stand in a warm place 1½ to 2 hours. Punch down and turn out on floured board and knead 2 or 3 minutes. Roll dough into one long sausage-like roll. Cut into 15 equal pieces. With your hands, pat each piece of dough into a ball, then roll out on floured board to measure 6-6½" in diameter and ¼" thick. Place each pita on a separate piece of aluminum foil and let stand in a warm place for one hour. Heat oven to 500°. Transfer foil with pita breads to lowest shelf of oven and bake 5 minutes or until breads start to brown and puff. Bake 4 breads at a time. Remove immediately and serve hot.

**FARMERS MARKET RECORDS
AND RADIOS — Stall #140-R**

River-Bottom Bread

This bread recipe from Western Frontier Moccasin & Leather is as much fun to eat as it is to make.

2 pkgs active dry
  yeast
½ cup warm water
½ cup chopped
  onion
3 tbs cooking oil
1 13-oz can (1-2/3
  cups) evaporated
  milk

¾ cup snipped
  parsley
3 tbs sugar
1 tsp salt
½ tsp dried dillweed
¼ tsp ground sage
¾ cup cornmeal
4 cups whole wheat
  flour

Soften yeast in ½ cup warm water. Cook onion in hot oil until tender and set aside until cool. Combine milk, parsley, sugar, salt, dillweed and sage and beat by hand or electric mixer. Add onion. Stir in yeast. Beat in cornmeal. Beat in ½ of the whole wheat flour. Add remaining flour to make a moderately soft dough. Turn out on lightly floured board. Knead 3 to 5 minutes until no longer sticky. Place in greased bowl, turning once to grease surface. Cover and let rise until double, about one hour in a warm place. Punch down; divide in half. Place in two well-greased 16-ounce coffee cans. Cover and let rise until double, 30 to 45 minutes. Bake in 350° oven for 45 minutes. Remove from tins and let cool on rack. Makes two loaves. Keeps well, wrapped in foil or plastic bag and stored in refrigerator or freezer.

**WESTERN FRONTIER MOCCASIN & LEATHER
Stall #150-17**

Not-So-Silly Dilly Bread

St. Moritz Bakery, creator of continental pastries, suggests this basic country bread.

1 pkg dry yeast
¼ cup warm water
1 cup creamed
  cottage cheese
  (room temper-
  ature)
2 tbs sugar
1 tbs instant minced
  onion
1 tbs butter
  (softened)
2 tbs dill seed
1 tsp salt
¼ tsp soda
1 egg, unbeaten
2¼-2½ cups flour,
  unsifted

Soften yeast in water. Combine cottage cheese, sugar, onion, butter, dill seed, soda, egg and yeast mixture. Add flour to make stiff dough. Cover and let rise until doubled (approximately one hour). Stir down and turn into loaf pan. Let rise in warm place about 30-40 minutes. Heat oven to 350°.
Brush top of bread dough with melted butter and coarse salt. Bake 30-40 minutes.

ST. MORITZ BAKERY — Stall #230

"Catalina" Cinnamon Rolls

Cake-decorating is the specialty you can watch in action at Humphrey's Bakery. They pass along this recipe for your enjoyment.

¾ **cup granulated sugar**
½ **lb lard or butter**
1 **cup boiling water**
2 **cakes yeast**
1 **cup cold water**
2 **eggs, beaten**
6 **cups flour**
1 **tsp salt**
¼ **lb margarine, melted**
1 **cup brown sugar, packed**
1 **cup nuts, chopped**
1 **cup raisins**

Cream together sugar and lard or butter. Add boiling water and mix thoroughly. Let cool. Dissolve yeast in cold water and combine with eggs. Add yeast mixture to sugar mixture and mix well. Add flour and salt to yeast mixture, cover bowl with a cloth and then store in refrigerator for one day (if you're in a hurry, chill in refrigerator for 2 hours). Divide dough in half and roll out on a well-floured board to ¼" thick. (Dough can be stored in well-covered bowl in refrigerator for 3-4 days.) Spread dough generously with melted margarine and sprinkle with brown sugar, nuts and raisins. Roll dough up, jelly-roll style, and cut in 2" wide strips. Place each slice cut side down in well-greased muffin tins and let stand covered with cloth for 2 hours in a warm place. Heat oven to 400°.
Bake 10-15 minutes. When slightly warm, glaze with icing.
Icing:
¾ **cup confectioners sugar**
approximately ⅛ **cup milk**
½ **tsp vanilla**

Combine all ingredients adding enough milk to make syrupy in texture.

HUMPHREY'S BAKERY — Stall #316

French Toast Oooh-la-la!

Chris' Coffee Shop knows exactly how to please breakfast appetites with this French Toast with "something extra."

½ cup half-and-half
3 eggs
salt
¼ tsp vanilla
¼ lb butter, or
  margarine
*6 slices egg
  bread
powdered sugar
maple or boysen-
  berry syrup
  (optional)

Whip half-and-half, eggs, salt and vanilla with wire whisk, or egg beater. Heat 3 tbs butter in skillet. Dip bread in egg mixture and coat thoroughly. Fry bread about 4 minutes each side, turning once, or until golden brown. Spoon a tsp melted butter on each piece of toast. Sprinkle with powdered sugar before serving. Makes 2 servings.

*For best results: egg bread should be sliced one inch thick then cut diagonally in half. Bread should be left out a day so that it is slightly dry.

CHRIS' COFFEE SHOP — Stall #412

No-Monkeying-Around Banana Bread

You'll go out on a limb for this moist and tasty bread from the Fun Shop, dispenser of toys, tricks and gag items.

½ cup margarine,
   or half butter and
   half margarine
¾ cup granulated
   sugar
2 eggs, beaten
½ tsp salt
1½ bananas,
   mashed
1¼ cups sifted
   flour
¾ tsp baking soda

Heat oven to 350°.
Combine margarine and sugar and blend thoroughly. Add eggs and salt and mix well. Add mashed bananas and continue to mix well. Sift together flour and baking soda and combine with banana mixture. Grease a small loaf pan and pour in mixture. Bake 30-40 minutes. Test in center for firmness; should bounce back at a touch.

FUN SHOP — Stall #140-M

"Azusa" Zucchini Bread

Du-Par's Bakery entices customers from miles around because they insist on using fresh fruits and vegetables for baking.

3 cups zucchini,
   unpeeled, grated
   medium
3 eggs, beaten
1 cup vegetable oil
2 cups sugar
3 cups flour
1 cup walnuts,
   chopped
1 cup coconut
2 tsp vanilla
1 tsp salt
1 tsp baking soda
1 tsp cinnamon
1 tsp baking powder

Heat oven to 325°.
Combine all ingredients and mix well. Pour mixture into 2 large, or 3 small, greased loaf pans. Bake for 1 hour or until light brown. Cool on rack.

DU-PARS BAKERY — Stall #110

"Pocahontas" Pumpkin Bread

Authentic Indian rugs, paintings and jewelry surround you at the Indian Trading Post, which suggests this bread for your next pow-wow.

2 2/3 cups sugar
2/3 cup shortening
4 eggs, beaten
1 1-lb can pumpkin
2/3 cup water
3 1/3 cups sifted
flour
½ tsp baking
powder
2 tsp baking soda
1½ tsp salt
1 tsp cinnamon
½ tsp nutmeg
1 cup walnuts,
chopped
1 cup dates,
chopped

Heat oven to 350°.
Cream together sugar and shortening until light and fluffy. Stir in eggs, pumpkin and water. Sift together dry ingredients and add gradually to pumpkin mixture. Add nuts and dates and blend well. Turn into 3 greased and floured (7¾ x 3⅝ x 2¼) loaf pans and bake for 1¼ hours or until a straw comes out clean.

INDIAN TRADING POST — Stall #140-1

SEAFOOD

"Hooray for Hollywood" Halibut

Serve this seafood entree on a platter from Koll's China House and watch the smiles of contentment.

**4 halibut steaks
(¾" thick)
salt and pepper
¾ cup sour cream
¼ cup fine dry bread
crumbs
¼ tsp garlic powder
1½ tbs chopped
chives
½ cup grated
Parmesan cheese
1 tsp paprika**

Heat oven to 400°.
Place halibut in a shallow, buttered baking dish, close-fitting. Sprinkle with salt and pepper. In bowl, mix sour cream, crumbs, garlic and chives. Spread over fish. Sprinkle with cheese, then paprika. Cover with aluminum foil and bake for 15-20 minutes. Remove foil and cook 5 additional minutes uncovered. Garnish with fresh parsley and lemon wedges. Makes 4 servings.

KOLL'S CHINA HOUSE — Stall #111

"Santa Monica" Swordfish

King's Half Sizes suggests a waist-watchers special, using low calorie fresh swordfish and a hint of Oriental seasonings.

**2 lbs swordfish
steaks
1/3 cup soy sauce
1 tsp grated lemon
peel
¼ cup fresh lemon
juice
1 clove garlic,
crushed
2 tsp prepared
mustard
½ cup salad oil
1 lemon, quartered**

Place fish in shallow baking dish side-by-side. Combine soy sauce, lemon peel, lemon juice, garlic, mustard and oil and blend well. Pour over swordfish and marinate several hours. Remove fish from marinade and place on heated broiler pan. Place under broiler 5 minutes on each side or until cooked through. Baste often with marinade. Serve with lemon wedges as garnish and fresh parsley. Makes 4-6 servings.

KING'S HALF SIZES — Stall #140-S

Cheesey Salmon Loaf

Cheeses from all over the world line the shelves of Farmers Market Cheese Shop. Try one of the Shop's "specials" for this dish.

- **1 1-lb can salmon, drained**
- **1 cup medium coarse cracker crumbs**
- **1 tbs onion, minced**
- **1 tsp celery seeds**
- **½ tsp salt**
- **⅛ tsp pepper**
- **1 egg, beaten**
- **2/3 cup evaporated milk**
- **2 tbs butter or margarine, melted**
- **1 cup cheddar cheese, grated**
- **2 eggs, hard cooked and shelled**

Flake salmon coarsely. Add cracker crumbs, onion, celery seeds, salt, pepper, egg, milk, butter and mix well. Spoon ½ of mixture into greased loaf pan; set the 2 hard cooked eggs tip to tip length-wise on the mixture. Spoon in remaining mixture and sprinkle cheese on top. Chill well.
Heat oven to 350°.
Bake loaf 35-40 minutes. Serve hot. Makes 4 servings.

**FARMERS MARKET CHEESE SHOP
Stall #236**

Bloomin' Good Pacific Salad

Altabet's Flower Shop creates fabulous floral arrangements that will grace any table serving this colorful crab entree.

- **½ lb mushrooms, sliced**
- **¼ lb butter or margarine**
- **1½ tbs shallots**
- **¼ cup flour**
- **1 qt half-and-half, hot**
- **salt and pepper to taste**
- **1½ tsp monosodium glutamate**
- **2 tsp rosemary**
- **½ cup sauterne**
- **2 lbs Alaskan king crab legs, cut in 3" pieces**

Saute mushrooms in 2 tbs of the butter until just tender. Add shallots and saute 2 additional minutes. Add flour and cook until smooth. Add half-and-half and simmer for 5 minutes. Add salt, pepper, monosodium glutamate, rosemary and sauterne. Saute crab in remaining butter, being careful not to break crab. Add sauce and simmer 3 minutes and remove from heat. Serve on plain rice. Makes 8 servings.

ALTABET'S FLOWER SHOP — Stall #328

Classic Fish & Chips

You've enjoyed dining on fish and chips at the Old English Fish & Chips stand; now try making them in your kitchen at home.

1 cup flour
¼ tsp salt
1 egg yolk
3 tbs milk
3 tbs water
2 tbs beer
1 egg white, stiffly beaten

1½ lbs halibut
salad oil or vegetable shortening

In a mixing bowl, blend together flour, salt, egg yolk, milk and water. Add beer. Gently mix in beaten egg white. Dip fish in batter.
Heat enough oil to cover fish, and fry fish until golden brown. Remove from pan and drain on paper towels. Makes 4 servings.

Chips (French Fries):

1½ lbs potatoes
salad oil or vegetable shortening

Peel potatoes and cut into lengthwise strips ¼" to ⅜" wide. Heat to 350° enough oil in skillet or deep frier to cover potatoes. Blanch potatoes by submerging in oil and partially cooking them. Remove and drain on paper towels. Return potatoes to hot oil and cook until golden brown. Makes 4 servings.

OLD ENGLISH FISH & CHIPS — Stall #312

Crafty Salmon Broil

Here's an artful method of preparing fresh salmon steaks suggested by Arts & Crafts by Vanity Studios.

4 tbs regular French salad dressing
2 tbs soy sauce
½ tsp ground ginger
4 salmon steaks
1 lime, thinly sliced

Combine salad dressing, soy sauce and ginger. Brush both sides of fish with mixture and place on a cookie sheet. Let stand 5 minutes. Broil 6 minutes, then gently turn fish over. Brush with any remaining sauce and broil second side for 4 to 6 minutes or until fish flakes when tested with fork. Garnish with lime slices. Makes 4 servings.

ARTS & CRAFTS BY VANITY STUDIOS
Stall #150-8

"No Postage Due" Gumbo

Farmers Market Post Office sent a special delivery request down South for this sensational soup.

4 slices bacon
½ lb okra, washed and cut into ½" slices
½ medium onion, diced
1 stalk celery, diced
1 or 2 cloves garlic, minced
½ lb mushrooms, sliced
1 16-oz can tomatoes
1-1½ cups water
2 bouillon cubes
salt and pepper to taste
dash of Worcestershire sauce
1 lb medium shrimp, peeled and cleaned

Cook bacon until crisp, drain and then place in a large kettle. Saute okra, onion, celery and garlic in bacon fat for about 10 minutes. Add this mixture to the bacon, then add mushrooms, tomatoes and water. Cook, stirring occasionally, for about 5 minutes. Dissolve bouillon cubes in ½ cup stock from the tomato mixture and return to pot. Add salt and pepper to taste and Worcestershire sauce. Simmer for 20 minutes, then add shrimp and continue simmering for 5 minutes. Serve hot gumbo over rice. Makes 4 servings.

FARMERS MARKET POST OFFICE

Fish Yucatan-Style

From the shelves of B. Dalton/Pickwick Bookshop comes this fabulous fish tale fit for a feast.

1 whole fish, such as pompano or snapper
juice of 1 lemon
salt and pepper to taste
4 tbs olive oil
1 onion, finely chopped
3 oz green olives, chopped
1 oz canned pimiento, chopped with liquid
1 tsp annatto (achiote)
2 tbs fresh cilantro, chopped or 2 tbs parsley, chopped
juice of 1 orange
2 hard-cooked eggs

Heat oven to 400°.
Marinate fish for 15 minutes in lemon juice, salt and pepper. Heat olive oil in a skillet and saute onion until limp. Add olives, pimiento and liquid, annatto, cilantro, salt and pepper. Cook for a few minutes and add orange juice. Put fish in buttered casserole, cover with sauce and cook for 30 minutes or until tender. Prepare garnish: separate hard-cooked eggs, yolks from whites. Press egg whites through a fine sieve in one bowl, then press yolk through a sieve in second bowl and set aside. When ready to serve fish, first sprinkle whites on fish then top with yolks.
(Note: In place of 1 whole fish, a filet per serving may be used.) Makes 6 servings.

B. DALTON PICKWICK

Flashy Curried Lobster

This festive dish, as developed by the Camera Exchange, is pretty as a picture.

1 onion, chopped
1 stalk celery, chopped
1 tart apple, chopped
1/3 cup butter or margarine
6 tbs flour
2 tbs curry powder
2 cups chicken broth
1 cup heavy cream
½ cup slivered almonds
3 cups lobster chunks

Saute onion, celery and apple in butter until tender but not browned. Stir in flour and curry powder. Add broth and cook and stir until sauce is smooth and boiling. Reduce heat. Pour cream in a steady slow stream, stirring constantly, until smooth. Add ¼ cup almonds and lobster, heat thoroughly. Spoon into serving dish and sprinkle with remaining almonds. Excellent served over steamed rice. Makes 6 servings.

CAMERA EXCHANGE — Stall #140-T

Psari Plaki
(Greek baked fish)

Gifts from 28 countries line the shelves at The International Shop; they've gone to Greece for this baked fish idea.

1 whole red
  snapper, striped
  bass, cod or
  whitefish (about
  4 lbs), cleaned
2 tsp salt
1 cup chopped
  green onions
2 tbs olive or
  vegetable oil
¼ cup chopped
  parsley
1 tsp grated lemon
  rind

½ tsp leaf oregano,
  crumbled
⅛ tsp pepper
2 tbs lemon juice
½ cup saltine
  cracker crumbs
4 tbs butter or
  margarine
¾ cup dry white
  wine
1 lemon, sliced
1 medium
  onion, sliced
2 small tomatoes,
  sliced

Heat oven to 350°.
Wash fish inside and out under cold water; pat dry with paper towel. Sprinkle fish inside and out with salt. Saute green onions 2 minutes in oil; stir in parsley, lemon rind, oregano, pepper & lemon juice. Spread half of onion mixture in bottom of baking dish or pan which will hold fish snugly. Put fish on top of onion mixture and spread remaining mixture on top of fish. Sprinkle with cracker crumbs, dot with butter or margarine. Pour wine into pan. Bake for 15 minutes and then arrange lemon and onion slices on top of fish and tomato slices along sides; brush with pan juices. Bake 20 minutes longer, or until fish flakes easily when tested with a fork. Garnish with parsley and lemon, if desired. Serve with pan juices spooned over. Makes 4-6 servings.

INTERNATIONAL SHOP — Stall #150-24

Breezy Bouillabaisse

A time-saving seafood recipe from the fashionable Today's Girl shop.

1 10½-oz can
   tomato vegetable
   soup
½ cup white wine
saffron, to taste
garlic powder, to
   taste
salt and pepper,
   to taste
12 clams in shell
¼ lb lobster meat,
   cooked
¼ lb crabmeat,
   cooked

Make soup according to directions on can. While soup is simmering, add wine, spices, seafood and cook until clam shells open. Serve in large tureen with garlic toast on the side. Makes 4 servings.

TODAY'S GIRL — Stall #140-N

Salmon Mousse

Transform the fresh salmon you'll find at Tusquellas Seafood into an elegant cold entree.

2 cups cold poached salmon	1 envelope unflavored gelatin
3 tbs lemon juice	½ cup cold water
3 tbs mayonnaise	½ cup heavy cream, whipped
1 tsp salt	
dash cayenne pepper	Cucumber Sauce

Mix cold salmon with lemon juice, mayonnaise, salt and cayenne pepper. In a saucepan sprinkle gelatin over cold water. Set over boiling water until dissolved. Combine gelatin and salmon mixture, fold in heavy whipped cream. Pour into a 1-quart mold and chill. Unmold on serving platter. Makes 6-8 servings.

To poach salmon:
**2 or 3 salmon steaks
   or fillets
water
½ cup dry white
   wine
2 sprigs of
   parsley
2 celery tops
salt and
   peppercorns**

Tie salmon in cheesecloth side by side and place in large pot. Just cover with water and add remaining ingredients. Poach gently, (bubbles should be very small) about 15-20 minutes, or until fish flakes easily. Remove from liquid and cool.

Cucumber Sauce:
**1 cup sour cream
2 tbs lemon juice
1 tsp prepared
   mustard
1 cup chopped
   cucumber, mixed a
   few seconds in
   blender
½ tsp each salt
   and onion powder**

Combine ingredients and chill. Spoon over each serving.

TUSQUELLAS SEAFOODS — Stall #138

Mendoza's Crusty Shrimp

While shopping for Mexican baskets and wrought iron, the Taxco Shop netted this shrimp dish.

**2 cups Masa Harina
   (or comparable
   corn flour)
¼ tsp salt
¼ tsp pepper
¼ tsp chili powder
1 12-oz can beer
1 quart cooking oil
2 lbs shrimp,
   cleaned and
   cooked**

Mix together corn flour, salt, pepper and chili powder. Add enough beer to make a thick batter. Let stand for 10 minutes at room temperature. Heat cooking oil in deep pan until boiling. Dip each shrimp into batter and drop into hot oil. When light golden brown, remove and drain on absorbent paper. After all shrimp are cooked, use any remaining batter by dropping spoonfuls of it into hot oil and cook for 5 minutes. Drain and serve with shrimp — these are called mendozas. Makes 4 servings.

TAXCO SHOP — Stalls #820-822

Mushroomed Mountain Trout

Vincent's Fine Foods serve short ribs, beef and ham. At home they suggest you try this trout.

**8 tbs butter or
   margarine, melted
½ lb fresh mush-
   rooms, sliced
salt and pepper
½ tsp sweet basil,
   crushed
2 tbs parsley,
   chopped
½ lemon, squeezed
4 trout, ½ lb each
½ cup dry white
   wine (optional)
1/3 cup bread
   crumbs, seasoned
4 scallions, minced
   fine
1 lemon, quartered**

Heat oven to 375°.
Melt 1 tbs butter in bottom of baking pan and cover bottom of pan with mushrooms. Season mushrooms with salt, pepper, ¼ tsp basil and 1 tbs parsley. Season trout with lemon juice, salt and pepper and remaining basil and parsley. Place trout on mushrooms and pour 2 tbs butter and wine over all. Sprinkle bread crumbs on trout and pour an additional 2 tbs butter over crumbs. Bake for 15 minutes or until bread crumbs are browned. Before serving, heat remaining butter and add scallions. When butter begins to foam, pour over fish. Serve a lemon wedge with each fish. Makes 4 servings.

VINCENT'S FINE FOODS — Stall #336

POULTRY

Make-Ahead Breakfast Casserole

Be prepared for rave reviews when you serve this make-ahead casserole, a bright breakfast idea from Jeri's Card Shop.

6-8 slices thin white bread with crusts cut off
1 12-oz pkg regular Jimmy Dean's sausage
1 tsp dry mustard
3 eggs, beaten
1¼ cups milk
¾ cup half-and-half
1¼ cups grated medium cheddar cheese
1 tsp salt
1 tsp Worcestershire sauce
dash of nutmeg

Fit bread to completely cover bottom of greased 9 x 13 pan. Brown sausage and pour off pan juices. Sprinkle mustard over sausage and stir. Beat eggs, add milk, half-and-half, cheese, salt, Worcestershire sauce and nutmeg. Blend with sausage. Pour over bread. Cover and refrigerate overnight.
Heat oven to 350°.
Bake casserole, uncovered, for 1 hour. Makes 8-10 servings.

JERI'S CARD SHOP — Stall #614

Poached Eggs "Pasadena"

The proprietors at the Egg Basket are "eggs-perts" in creating interesting menus with their fabulous assortment of eggs.

8 strips bacon
2 tbs flour
1 tsp monosodium glutamate
1 13-oz can evaporated milk
1 cup water
2 tbs Worcestershire sauce
dash of Tabasco sauce
salt and white pepper to taste
½ lb Old English cheese
8 fresh eggs
8 slices egg bread, toasted

Fry bacon crisp — remove from pan to drain. Stir flour into bacon grease (don't brown). Add milk and water and continue stirring. Add seasonings and cheese. Stir till smooth. Simmer 10 minutes. Add eggs one at a time — cover and simmer 8 to 10 minutes. To serve, place toast on plate and spoon over egg mixture. Top with 2 bacon strips. Makes 4 servings.

EGG BASKET — Stall #222

Breakfast Italian Style

Start the day the Italian way with a warm artichoke antipasto from Tony's Pizza & Spaghetti.

2 tbs olive oil
16 small artichokes
   (raw or canned,
   drained)
8 eggs
Parmesan cheese
salt and pepper
   to taste
1 can green peas,
   drained
2 tbs fresh parsley,
   chopped fine

Heat oil in large skillet. Clean and slice artichokes and fry for 5 minutes. Beat eggs, mix with cheese, salt, pepper and peas. Pour over artichokes and cook for 3 minutes, stirring constantly. Serve on heated platter, sprinkle top with parsley. Delicious with crusty Italian bread. Makes 4 servings.

TONY'S PIZZA - SPAGHETTI — Stall #310

Chicken Pastel
(chicken in crust)

Gourmets will love the handy accessories from the Gadget Nook to make cooking assignments like this chicken all the easier.

pie crust
1 2½ to 3 lb chicken
juice of 1 lemon
3 tbs soy sauce
5 cups water
salt and pepper
   to taste
1 chorizo (Spanish
   sausage)

2 eggs, hard cooked
   and sliced
1 4-oz can Vienna
   sausage
6 tbs butter or
   margarine
1 16-oz can peas,
   drained

Heat oven to 375°.
Make pie crust dough, wrap in plastic wrap and refrigerate. Bone and skin chicken and cut into small pieces. Put chicken in a bowl and add lemon juice and soy sauce. Let stand for 15 minutes. In a saucepan, simmer chicken, water, salt and pepper until meat is tender and most of liquid has evaporated. Fry the chicken and chorizo in butter until brown. Place chicken and all sauce in casserole. Arrange sliced eggs, peas and Vienna sausage on top of chicken. Remove pie crust dough from refrigerator and roll out on floured board to fit top of casserole. Cover top with pie crust, pressing edges well to insure a good seal. Bake until crust is golden brown, about 12 minutes. Makes 6 servings.

GIFT AND GADGET NOOK — Stall #112

Cacciatore-Like Chicken

Of all the delectable Italian foods that come from Yolanda's, this recipe is one of the best.

2 3 to 4 lb chickens,
   cut into eighths

½ cup soy sauce
½ cup sauterne wine

Heat oven to 400°.
Brush each piece of chicken with soy sauce and bake in oven for 40 minutes to an hour or until chicken is golden. Baste regularly with juices. Remove from oven and degrease. Pour sauterne over chicken, place pan on burner and rotate pan burning off the alcohol and browning the chicken, approximately 3 to 4 minutes. Pour sauce over chicken and return to oven to warm through. Serve with rice or noodles. Makes 6 to 8 servings.
Sauce:

1 10½-oz can
   mushrooms,
   drained and
   sliced
1 oz butter
1 tsp onion juice
1 tsp Worcestershire
   sauce
3 tbs arrowroot
   (dilute in 3 tbs
   cold chicken

   broth or water)
2 cups unsalted
   chicken broth
1 7-oz can tomatoes
   with green
   peppers
pinch of nutmeg
1 tsp thyme,
   crushed
salt to taste

Combine all ingredients in a saucepan and cook over low heat until all flavors are blended or about 15 minutes.

YOLANDA'S ITALIAN KITCHEN — Stall #738

Apple-Stuffed "Pabo" (turkey)

This turkey wears a different dressing — one with tart and juicy apples, from Mort's Restaurant.

Dressing for 18 lb. turkey:

4 tbs margarine or vegetable oil
2 tart apples, chopped
1 medium onion, chopped
4 to 6-oz dried fruit, cut into pieces
1½ cups celery, chopped
2 lbs dry white or corn bread
salt and pepper
1 tbs thyme, crushed
1½ tsp sage
water, chicken broth or white wine
¼ lb butter or margarine

Heat oil in large skillet. Add apple, onion, fruit and celery. Saute until tender. Break bread into very small cubes and add to above mixture with seasonings. Add enough water or broth or wine to hold together and mix well.
Prepare turkey:
Heat oven to 375°.
Wash turkey inside and out and rub with ¼ lb butter or margarine mixed with salt, pepper and paprika. Stuff with dressing and truss. Place on rack back side down; cover with aluminum foil and bake 25 minutes per lb. Baste frequently with drippings.

MORT'S — Stall #742

Tipsy Turkey Marsala

Saunders Poultry has cooked up a novel method to use turkey parts.

3 turkey thighs and legs
salt and pepper to taste
1 tbs tarragon, crushed
3 tbs chicken fat, butter or margarine
3 large onions, sliced thin
3 carrots, peeled and sliced
3 stalks celery, sliced with tops
1 parsnip, peeled and sliced
3 sprigs parsley, chopped
1 cup Marsala wine

Heat oven to 400°.
Separate thighs and legs. Season with salt, pepper and tarragon. Melt chicken fat in roaster and add onions, carrots, celery, parsnip and parsley. Cook until just tender. Place turkey on vegetables and cover roaster (aluminum foil can be used to cover). Cook for 30 minutes at 400°, then lower heat to 350° for an additional 30 minutes. Remove foil and baste with wine, turning pieces. Cook for another hour, basting every 15 minutes. Makes 3-6 servings.

SAUNDERS POULTRY — Stall #18

Glossy Cornish Game Hen

Right off the ranch are the fresh birds at Puritan Poultry, like the cornish hens you'll use in this delicious main course.

1 pkg Rice-a-Roni brown and wild rice mix
½ cup canned mushrooms, chopped
½ cup celery, chopped
½ cup onions, chopped
all giblets from hens except necks, chopped (optional)
½ cup butter or margarine, melted
½ tsp ground sage
½ cup chicken stock
6 game hens, washed
¼ lb butter or margarine, soft
1 tbs seasoned salt
1 tbs seasoned pepper
1 cup white wine (optional)
½ cup orange juice
½ cup currant jelly

Heat oven to 350°.
Prepare Rice-a-Roni according to directions on package, but do not cook away all liquid. In a separate skillet, saute mushrooms, celery, onions and giblets in melted butter. Add sage, half of the salt, pepper and chicken stock. Cook slowly on low heat for 10 minutes. Combine mushroom mixture and rice and mix well. Should this rice mixture seem dry, add more chicken stock. Stuff hens with rice mixture and truss. Rub each hen with softened butter and sprinkle with remaining salt and pepper. Place in a foil-lined pan, basted with wine and cover. Cook 45 minutes. Combine orange juice and jelly and melt. Brush hens with this glaze and return to oven uncovered 10-15 additional minutes. Serve immediately. Makes 6 servings.

PURITAN POULTRY — Stall #226

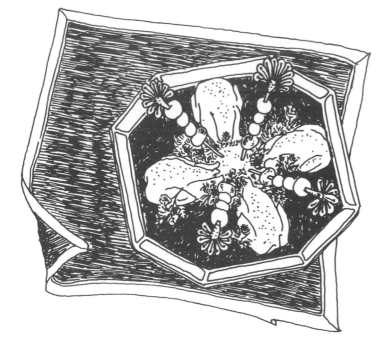

Chinese Chicken Cashew

The chefs at Magee's Deli are as famous for their corned beef as they are for fabulous foreign fare.

2 lbs chicken breasts
2 tbs cornstarch
4 tbs soy sauce
4 tbs vegetable oil
1 cup raw cashew
   nuts
2 stalks celery,
   sliced thin
½ lb snow peas
¼ lb fresh mush-
   rooms, sliced

1 large onion, sliced
   thin
½ green pepper,
   sliced thin
1 clove garlic

Sauce:
1 cup chicken broth
2 tsp cornstarch
salt and pepper to
   taste

Remove skin and bones from chicken breasts and slice into thin strips. Place chicken in a bowl with cornstarch and soy sauce and set aside while preparing the vegetables. Heat 2 tbs oil in wok or large skillet. Add cashews. Stir with wooden spoon for 30 seconds until nuts are lightly roasted. Remove nuts. Add 2 tsp oil to pan. When hot add chicken mixture; stir fry until chicken is done (about 2 minutes); turn out into dish. Reheat pan with more oil. Toss in vegetables and stir fry until tender crisp. Return chicken to pan with vegetables and sauce made of blend of broth and corn- starch. Cook, stirring constantly until sauce thickens. Add salt and pepper to taste. Add cashews, reserving a few for garnish on top when served with rice. Makes 4 servings.

MAGEE'S DELICATESSEN — Stall #220

"La Cienega" Chestnut Dressing

The crunchiness of fresh chestnuts adds an Oriental dimension to this dressing from the specialists at House of Chestnuts.

Stuffing for 20-pound turkey:

3 large loaves dry
   bread, cubed
   (7 quarts)
½ lb butter, melted
1 tsp cinnamon
1 tsp nutmeg
½ tsp sage
½ tsp salt
½ tsp pepper
½ cup fresh parsley,
   snipped

3 large onions,
   chopped
2 cups celery,
   chopped
4 apples, pared
   and chopped
3 cups water
2 cups chestnuts,
   blanched and
   coarsely chopped

In large roaster pan, melt butter. Add bread, seasonings, parsley and nuts — set aside. Place onions, celery and apples in water and simmer until about 1/3 done (tender, but with shape.) Add wet ingredients to the dry. Stir. The mixture should be quite dry. (Pick up a handful, squeeze lightly to form a ball and drop back into roaster pan — it should break apart when it falls.) If not moist enough, add more water. Pack lightly into salted cavity of bird. (Any leftover dressing may be baked in a well- covered casserole for 1 hour.)

HOUSE OF CHESTNUTS — Stall #708

Chicken a la Queen

This chicken entree, furnished by the owners of Farmers Market — A.F. Gilmore Co., majestically turns plain poultry into a royal repast.

4 chicken breasts, skinned and boned	½ lb mushrooms, sliced
6 tbs butter or margarine	1 cup sour cream
1½ cups dry white wine	salt and pepper to taste
1 small onion, diced	1 8½-oz can artichoke hearts, drained

Saute chicken breasts in 4 tbs melted butter until lightly browned. Pour over chicken ¾ cup of wine and cover. Cook about 25-35 minutes. Heat oven to 300°.
In a separate pan, cook onions and mushrooms in remaining butter until tender. Stir in balance of wine and sour cream. Stir constantly on low heat, making sure cream does not curdle. Place chicken in greased casserole and season with salt and pepper. Place artichoke hearts and mushrooms around chicken and pour in all sauce. Warm in oven before serving. Makes 4 servings.

A.F. GILMORE COMPANY

Souper Chicken

You'll win yourself a bouquet of compliments with this Cedric's Flower Shop recipe for an elegant and super chicken.

1 cup raw rice	1 cup dry white wine
1 10½-oz can chicken with rice soup	1 3 to 4 lb chicken, cut up or equivalent parts of your choice
1 10½-oz can cream of celery soup	
1 10½-oz can cream of mushroom soup	1 2¾-oz pkg slivered almonds

Heat oven to 325°.
In a large shallow unbuttered glass baking dish, place the uncooked rice and smooth evenly over the bottom. In a saucepan, combine the soups (undiluted) and wine. Warm, stirring until completely blended. Pour half of the soup-wine mixture evenly over the rice. Place the chicken parts, skin-side up, evenly over the rice. Pour remaining soup-wine mixture over chicken. Spread slivered almonds over the top. Bake for 1½ hours or until chicken is tender. Makes 6-8 servings.

CEDRIC'S FLOWER SHOP — Stall #826

Gedempte Chicken & Meat Balls

Want to cure those menu blues? Gellman's Pharmacy has just the prescription for a new and better way to serve chicken.

1 lb brown sugar
4 lemons, juiced
1 6-oz can tomato puree
1 8-oz can tomato sauce
2½ cups chicken bouillon
½ box white raisins, washed
garlic salt to taste
onion salt to taste
9 chicken legs
9 chicken thighs
3 chicken breasts
4 lbs ground meat
4 slices pumpernickel bread, crusts removed
2 medium lemons, juiced
1 tbs sugar
salt and pepper to taste
1 tbs prepared mustard
2 tbs ketchup
garlic salt
onion salt
½ cup cold water

In a large pot combine sugar, lemon juice, tomato puree, tomato sauce, raisins, garlic and onion salts, and mix well. Add chicken parts and mix thoroughly. Cook over low heat for one hour. Prepare meatballs by soaking pumpernickel bread in lemon juice, sugar and seasonings until all liquid is absorbed. Add meat and mix thoroughly with water. Shape meat into 1" diameter balls and add to chicken. Cook an additional 35 minutes. Serve over noodles or plain rice. Makes 10-12 servings.

GELLMAN'S PHARMACY — Stall #134

Sicilian Turkey Parmigiana

Roger's Poultry, whose wares reflect true ranch fresh flavor, show us a new way with turkey.

2 lbs turkey cutlets, ¼" thick
1 egg, beaten
¼ tsp salt
dash of pepper
¾ cup bread crumbs
5 tbs Parmesan cheese, grated
olive oil or shortening
1 8-oz can tomato sauce
½ lb mozzarella cheese, sliced thin
oregano

Heat oven to 350°.
Have cutlets pounded and dip into egg which has been seasoned with salt and pepper. Then dip into a combination of bread crumbs, 3 tbs of the Parmesan cheese, and dash of oregano. Saute cutlets in oil or shortening until well browned. Place in a shallow baking dish. Pour tomato sauce over cutlets, then top with slices of mozzarella cheese. Sprinkle with remaining Parmesan cheese. Bake about 55-60 minutes. Makes 6 servings.

**ROGERS FARMERS MARKET POULTRY
Stall #216**

"Malibu" Mulligatawny

The wide assortment of ingredients in this East Indian Stew is second only to the hundreds of notions at Farmers Market Variety Store.

1 3 lb chicken, cut into eighths
¼ cup fat or vegetable oil
¼ cup onion, chopped
¼ cup carrots, sliced
½ green pepper, chopped
1 tbs parsley, chopped

2 tart apples, sliced
1 tbs flour
1 tsp curry powder
2 whole cloves
1 tsp sugar
1 16-oz can tomatoes, including liquid
salt and pepper to taste
4 qts cold water

In an 8 qt pot, brown chicken and onions, carrots, green pepper, parsley and apples. Add flour, curry powder, cloves and sugar and blend thoroughly. Add tomatoes and water and cook slowly until chicken is tender, about 30 to 40 minutes. Remove chicken, cut into smaller pieces and set aside. Strain liquid into a large bowl and rub vegetables through sieve or pour liquid and vegetables in blender and blend, first removing cloves. Return liquid and chicken to pot, add salt and pepper to taste. Before serving, heat thoroughly. Makes 6-8 servings.

FARMERS MARKET VARIETY STORE
Stall #616

Venetian Chicken n' Shrimp

This unique recipe reflects the out-of-the-ordinary jewelry and gift items available at the Glass Blower.

1 2½ to 3 lb broiler-fryer chicken, cut up	¼ lb butter or margarine
salt and pepper to taste	Italian sauce
	1 lb cleaned raw shrimp

Season chicken with salt and pepper. Brown slowly in butter, turning once. Add sauce, cover and simmer until chicken is tender, about 45 minutes. Add shrimp, being sure to immerse in sauce. Cover and continue cooking until shrimp are done, about 5 to 10 minutes. Serve in hot soup bowls. Pass warm french bread for dunking. Makes 4 servings.

Italian Sauce:

2 8-oz cans tomato sauce	3 tbs parsley, chopped
½ cup cooking Claret	1 tsp sweet basil
¾ cup onion, chopped	1 bay leaf, crushed
1 clove garlic, chopped	½ tsp salt
	dash pepper

Combine all ingredients and cook for 15 minutes.

GLASS BLOWER — Stall #140-K

Sweet & Sour Chicken

Farmers and city folk alike appreciate chicken with a special sauce, like this idea from Chuck's Place.

1 3 to 4 lb chicken or 4 chicken breasts	½ tsp pepper
4 tbs cornstarch or flour	2 tbs water
2 egg yolks	1 tsp salt
	2 cups oil (for deep frying)

Cut chicken in approximately 2" size pieces. Mix thoroughly 2 tbs cornstarch, 2 egg yolks, water, salt and pepper. Dip each piece of the chicken in this mixture, then roll each piece in the remaining cornstarch until well coated. Fry chicken in deep fat about 6-8 minutes or until slightly brown. Remove from the oil.

Sweet & Sour Sauce:

2½ tbs vinegar	3 tbs Worcestershire sauce
4 tbs sugar	2 drops food coloring
4 tbs ketchup	1 tbs cornstarch (diluted with 1 tbs water)
3 tbs water	
½ tsp salt	
1 tbs lemon juice	
1 tbs oil	

Bring to boil the vinegar, sugar, ketchup, water, salt, lemon juice, Worcestershire sauce and food coloring. Add a small amount of thin cornstarch paste. Cook until sauce becomes transparent. Add oil and stir for 1 minute. Put fried chicken back into the sauce mixture, stir until hot. Makes 4 servings.

CHUCK'S PLACE — Stall #150-25

MEATS

Premiere Tamale Pie

You'll dig this Mexican-style perennial from Pitt's Garden Shop.

2 cups milk
1¾ cups yellow corn
  meal
2 large onions,
  chopped
¼ cup oil (or olive
  oil)
3 eggs, lightly
  beaten
1 medium green bell
  pepper, chopped
1 lb ground beef

½ lb ground salt or
  fresh pork
1 17-oz can whole
  corn, drained
1 16-oz can
  tomatoes, drained
1 pt ripe olives,
  pitted
1 cup raisins, white
  or black
2 tsp chili powder
salt and pepper
  to taste

Heat oven to 350°.
Combine milk and corn meal and let stand about 15 minutes. Saute onions in oil until clear. Add eggs and bell pepper to milk mixture. Mix well. Add meat and mix well. Add corn, tomatoes, olives, raisins, chili powder, salt and pepper and mix well. Remove onions from oil with slotted spoon and add to corn mixture. Pour mixture into large baking pan and bake for 1½ hours. Makes 8-10 servings.

PITT'S GARDEN SHOP — Stall #818

Elegant Liver & Mushrooms

Farmers Market Beauty Salon staff creates stylish cuisine as well as coiffures, such as this flavorful liver.

¼ lb sweet butter or
  margarine
1½ large onions,
  sliced thin
½ lb mushrooms,
  quartered
1 tbs tarragon
juice of ½ lemon
¾ cup flour
2 eggs, beaten
2 tbs milk
1 lb calves liver

Saute onions and mushrooms in butter. Add tarragon and lemon juice and cook until tender. Drain and set aside. Place flour, salt and pepper on a plate. In another bowl, combine eggs and milk and mix thoroughly. Dip liver in eggs and then flour. Using butter from onions and mushrooms, fry liver on low heat, adding butter if necessary. Cook liver 10 minutes on each side turning once. To insure that liver is cooked all the way through, cut into it occasionally. Add onions and mushrooms to pan to reheat before serving. Makes 2-4 servings.

**FARMERS MARKET BEAUTY SALON
Stall #150-34**

Super Slumgullion

It doesn't take the mechanical expertise offered at Farmers Market Automotive to create this delicious entree made from leftovers.

1 lb ground beef
1 lb ground pork
salt and pepper to
   taste
1 tbs oregano
2 tbs butter or
   margarine
2 green bell
   peppers, diced
3 medium onions,
   diced
1 stalk celery, diced
1 6-oz pkg wide
   noodles

salted water
1 17-oz pkg frozen
   small peas,
   thawed
1 16-oz can
   tomatoes, drained
1 can cream of
   mushroom soup
1 lb grated cheddar
   cheese
1 4½-oz can ripe
   olives, sliced
2 tsp curry powder

Heat oven to 350°.
Salt a skillet and brown beef and pork. Drain excess fat. Add salt, pepper and crushed oregano. Set aside. Melt butter and lightly brown peppers, onions and celery and add to meat mixture. Cook noodles according to directions on package in salted water, "al dente," (firm) and drain off water. Mix together all remaining ingredients, reserving ½ tablespoon of cheese and combine with meat and noodles. Place in large baking pan and top with remaining cheese. Bake uncovered for 45 minutes. Makes 6-8 servings.

FARMERS MARKET AUTOMOTIVE CENTER

German Beef Mit Sauerkraut

Magee's Kitchen contributes a hearty dish, straight from the shores of the Rhine River.

3 to 4 lbs beef
   brisket
1 cup water
1 medium onion,
   quartered
2 tsp salt
¼ tsp pepper
1 tsp caraway seeds
2 tbs cider or wine
   vinegar
2 bay leaves
2 tbs brown sugar
1 large potato
2 lbs sauerkraut

Brown meat slowly in its own fat, or add small amount of shortening. Pour off drippings. Add water, onion, salt, pepper, caraway seeds, vinegar and bay leaves. Cover and simmer 3 hours or until tender. Discard bay leaves. Add sugar. Pare potato and shred medium fine. Add to meat along with sauerkraut. Cover and cook 30 minutes more. Makes 8-10 servings.

MAGEE'S KITCHEN — Stall #624

Ox-Tail Stew-pendous

The flavorful stew you'll reap from this recipe from La Frieda Meats is well worth the time it takes to simmer.

2 tbs margarine
2 onions, chopped
2 lbs ox-tails
salt and pepper
  to taste
1 28-oz can
  tomatoes
1 10½-oz can
  tomato soup
1 cup water
1 lb carrots, peeled
6 potatoes, peeled
½ stalk celery,
  cleaned
1 tbs oregano
1 tsp parsley flakes
1 bay leaf

Using a large pot, melt margarine and saute onions until clear. Add ox-tails, salt and pepper, and brown on all sides. Add tomatoes, tomato soup and water, and cook covered one hour over low heat. Add carrots, potatoes and celery all cut in large pieces. Add oregano, parsley and bay leaf and continue cooking until meat is tender, about 2½ hours. Makes 4 servings.

LA FRIEDA MEATS — Stall #120

Cidery Ham

See the wizards at work at Langston's Sausage Shop where sausages are made from scratch.

10-lb ham
½ tsp ground cloves
1 tsp cinnamon
½ tsp ginger
1 tsp dry mustard
½ tsp paprika
½ cup flour
½ cup water
apple cider
1 beaten egg
½ cup brown sugar
½ cup bread crumbs
3 tbs minced parsley

Heat oven to 275°.
Wash and dry ham. Over the fleshy side, sprinkle cloves, cinnamon, ginger, mustard and paprika. Combine flour and water to make a paste-like mixture. Cover ham with flour paste. Place skin side down in baking pan and fill pan ¾ full with cider. Bake 3 hours. Remove paste and rind. Bake fat side up for 1 hour, basting frequently with pan juices. Brush fat surface with beaten egg. Mix brown sugar, crumbs and parsley and sprinkle on ham. Continue baking until brown. Remove ham and slice. Add cider or water to drippings in pan to make gravy. Makes 16-18 servings.

LANGSTON'S SAUSAGE — Stall #428

Wandering Gypsy Stew

Taken from the days when gypsy bands were still a familiar part of the European scene. Their nomadic life necessitated the meal-in-one, a combination of meats, vegetables and spices cooked in a pot over the campfires, as offered by Magliano Jewelry Shop.

1 lb lean beef flank, cut into 1" cubes
1 lb boned pork shoulder, cut into 1" cubes
1 lb veal or lamb, cut into 1" cubes
1 2-lb chicken, boned, skinned and cut into large pieces
2 carrots, peeled and cut into large pieces
2 stalks celery, cut into large pieces
3 small onions
2 medium green peppers, cut into large pieces
2 to 4 small hot red peppers, seeded and chopped fine
½ cup flour
1 tsp paprika
1 pinch cayenne pepper
1 bay leaf
3 cloves
salt and pepper to taste
2 tbs tomato paste
2 potatoes, peeled and cubed
2 fresh tomatoes, peeled and diced
1/3 cup fresh parsley, chopped

Heat oven to 325°.
Quickly brown the beef, veal and pork cubes and chicken pieces in hot fat in a sizeable pot. Add carrots and celery, onions and peppers and the flour. Mix well and let ingredients sweat for 5 minutes. Cover with water (beef or chicken stock is preferred). Add all the spices, including the hot red pepper and tomato paste. Let simmer for 15 minutes. Now add the potatoes, cover and finish cooking in the oven for approximately 45 minutes or until the meat and potatoes are tender. For the finishing touch, add the tomatoes and chopped parsley — mix and serve. Makes 6-8 servings.

MAGLIANO JEWELRY SHOP — Stall #718

"Balboa" Beef Bourguignon

Farmers Market Wine Shop features domestic and imported wines from the world's finest vineyards. Try a Burgundy in this dish.

2 tbs oil	1 bay leaf
5 onions, sliced	½ cup bouillon
2 lbs beef, cubed	1 cup red wine
1½ tbs flour	½ lb fresh mush-
1 tsp marjoram	rooms, sliced
1 tsp thyme	additional bouillon
½ tsp pepper	and wine, as
½ tsp salt	needed

Heat oil in large heavy deep pot or dutch oven. Add sliced onions and cook until tender. Remove and set aside. Sprinkle meat with flour seasoned with half of the salt and pepper. Saute beef cubes until browned. Add marjoram, thyme, salt and pepper. Add bouillon and wine (1 part stock to 2 parts wine) as necessary to keep beef covered. Return onions to pot after meat has cooked 2 hours or until meat is tender. Add mushrooms and stir. Cook 30 minutes longer. (Add bouillon and wine mixture if necessary.) Makes 6 servings.

FARMERS MARKET WINE SHOP — Stall #326

Miracle Make-Ahead Marinade

Feed-Rite Pet Shop has the formula for a make-ahead marinade to add a real outdoor flavor to your next meal.

1 tbs parsley, either flakes or chopped	1 clove garlic, minced
1 tbs onion flakes	½ cup sherry
1 tbs powdered mushrooms	½ cup rum
½ tbs smoke flavor	¼ cup soy sauce
½ tsp sweet basil, crushed	½ cup salad oil
1 tsp oregano, crushed	1 20-oz bottle ketchup
1 tsp marjoram	1/3 cup A-1 sauce
	2/3 cup Worcester-shire sauce

Combine all ingredients and mix thoroughly. Chill. May be stored in refrigerator for several weeks. Marinate steak or other meat 2-4 hours before cooking.

FEED-RITE PET SHOP — Stall #720

Oriental Stir-Fried Beef

The farm-fresh vegetables from Farmers Market Fruit and Produce enhance this authentic stir-fry beef specialty.

2 lbs chuck beef or
   seven bone roast
1½ tbs soy sauce
1 tsp monosodium
   glutamate
½ tsp sugar
dash of pepper
1 tbs sherry
½ tsp fresh ginger,
   grated
4 drops sesame
   seed oil
1 tbs peanut oil
¼ tsp salt
1 clove garlic,
   crushed
6 medium mush-
   rooms, sliced
1 medium onion,
   sliced
¼ cup water
1 tbs cornstarch
chives

Slice beef very thin, against grain, in strips. Place in bowl and add 1 tbs soy sauce, monosodium glutamate, sugar, pepper, sherry, ginger and sesame oil. Mix well. Heat peanut oil in large skillet or wok and add salt and garlic. Stir in mushrooms and onions and cook until onions are tender. Lift out meat from marinade and add to mushroom mixture, stirring constantly for 2 minutes. Do not over-cook. Add water and stir until boiling. Mix together cornstarch and remaining soy sauce and make into a smooth paste. Add to pan and stir until gravy thickens. Serve over rice. Sprinkle each individual serving with chives. Makes 4 servings.

FARMERS MARKET FRUIT AND PRODUCE
Stall #144

Hamburger Country Pie

Put your sights on this dish — target of many awards from Milleson's Sporting Goods

Crust:
½ cup tomato sauce
½ cup bread crumbs
¼ cup onions, chopped
½ tsp salt
⅛ tsp pepper
1 lb hamburger
⅛ tsp oregano

Combine all above ingredients, mix well and pat into 9" pie pan. Flute edges.

Filling:
1-1/3 cup cooked rice
1 cup water
½ tsp salt
1 12-oz can tomato sauce
1 cup cheddar cheese, grated

Heat oven to 350°.
Combine rice, water, salt, sauce and ½ cup cheese. Spoon into meat shell. Cover with foil and bake for 25 minutes. Remove foil, sprinkle top with remaining ½ cup cheese and bake 10 to 15 minutes longer. Makes 6 servings.

MILLESON'S SPORTING GOODS — Stall #140

Pork Chops Verdura

Scissors experts from the Barber Shop snip and pass along this tonsorial palate pleaser.

**4 pork chops, cut ½"
  thick
salt and pepper
1 tbs olive oil
1 10½-oz can
  chicken broth
1 15½-oz jar Ragu
  spaghetti sauce
1 medium onion,
  thinly sliced**

**1 medium green
  pepper, cut in
  strips
¾ cup converted
  rice, uncooked
½ cup olives, sliced
2 cups zucchini,
  thinly sliced**

Heat oven to 350°.
Season chops with salt and pepper and brown on both sides in olive oil in large skillet. Spoon off fat. Stir in chicken broth, spaghetti sauce, onion and green pepper. Bring to a boil and reduce heat. Continue cooking, covered, for 15 minutes. Stir in rice and olives. Cover and cook 30 minutes. Uncover and place zucchini on top and continue cooking, covered, an additional 15 minutes. Makes 3-4 servings.

BARBER SHOP — Stall #750

Pork Chops Teriyaki

The succulent pork products from Farmers Market Pork Shop are the inspiration for this main dish.

**6 pork rib or loin
  chops, cut 1¼"
  thick
¾ cup soy sauce
¼ cup lemon juice
1 tbs chili sauce
1 tbs brown sugar
1 clove garlic,
  minced
½ tsp ginger, grated
  (optional)**

Arrange pork chops in glass baking dish. Combine remaining ingredients and mix well. Pour over chops and cover with aluminum foil. Marinate 3 to 6 hours, or overnight, in refrigerator, turning chops occasionally.
Set oven to broiling temperature. Place chops on rack on broiler pan and place in oven about 5 inches from heat. Broil 12 to 15 minutes each side, basting with marinade. Makes 3-4 servings.

FARMERS MARKET PORK SHOP — Stall #114

Sterling Short Ribs

These short ribs are worthy of serving on one of David Orgell's fabulous assortment of sterling and silverplate accessories.

1½ tsp salt
½ tsp pepper
3 to 4 lbs beef
   short ribs
1 8-oz can tomato
   sauce
2 tbs molasses
2 tbs cider vinegar
1 tbs onion, minced

Heat oven to 275°.
Sprinkle salt and pepper on all sides of short ribs and place in a 3-quart casserole and set aside. In a small pan, combine tomato sauce, molasses, vinegar and onions and bring to a boil, stirring constantly. Pour over ribs. Cover with aluminum foil or lid and bake 3 to 4 hours or until tender. Remove from oven and cool. Refrigerate overnight. Remove from refrigerator and defat. When at room temperature, return to 350° oven and reheat about 30 minutes or until thoroughly heated. Makes 4 servings.

DAVID ORGELL — Stall #150-38

Fancy Pants Lamb

Your lamb will look even lovelier when dressed in fancy pants, according to the proprietor at Pants World.

½ cup soy sauce
½ tsp fresh grated
   ginger (or ground
   ginger)
¼ tsp dry mustard
2 cloves garlic,
   crushed
½ tsp thyme
½ tsp rosemary
¼ cup vegetable oil
2 lamb racks

Combine all ingredients in blender or bowl except lamb racks and blend thoroughly. Make a cut about 1½" down the thin part of each lamb rib bone. Place lamb racks in pan and pour marinade over. Refrigerate overnight.
Heat oven to 400°.
Place lamb on broiler pan and place in center of oven. Cook 45 minutes, basting at least 4 times during cooking with the marinade. Before serving, cut into ribs or serve whole; place a "paper pant" or sleeve on each rib bone. Makes 6-8 servings.

PANT WORLD — Stall #150-12

Kebobs by Candlelight

Enhance your supper table with Candles by Drew to turn a simple dinner into an elegant occasion.

¼ cup salad oil
2 tbs cider vinegar
1 tsp celery salt
1 tsp onion salt
¾ tsp garlic salt
¾ tsp oregano
  leaves, crushed
½ tsp salt

½ tsp ground black
  pepper
2 lbs boneless
  shoulder or top
  round of beef
8 medium size
  mushrooms caps
2 zucchini, cut into
  ½" pieces

Combine oil, vinegar, celery salt, onion salt, garlic salt, oregano, salt and pepper in saucepan. Heat to boiling point and cool. Cut meat into 1½" cubes and add to marinade with mushrooms and zucchini. Toss lightly. Cover and marinate 4 to 6 hours, turning occasionally to season uniformly. Dip skewers into marinade. Alternate meat and vegetables on skewers. Place on grill over a bed of medium-slow burning coals. Cook 20 to 25 minutes, turning and basting frequently. Kebobs may be broiled in oven 4" to 6" from heat source for 8 to 10 minutes.

CANDLES BY DREW — Stall #150-31

Chinatown Pork
(sweet and sour)

Sweet and sour sauce originated in China, but it's popular now worldwide — especially at Peking Kitchen.

2 lbs pork
1 tbs dry sherry
1 tsp salt
4 tsp cornstarch
1 8-oz can pineapple chunks (including juice)
½ cup sweet mixed pickle chunks
2 medium tomatoes, peeled and seeded
1 small green pepper, seeded
2 cloves garlic, crushed
4 tbs vegetable oil
2 tbs soy sauce
2 tbs sugar
1 tbs vinegar

Cut pork into 1" cubes, trim fat. Mix with sherry, salt and 2 teaspoon of cornstarch in medium size bowl and set aside. Drain pineapple and sweet pickle and save juice. Cut tomatoes into wedges; cut green pepper into chunks. Heat garlic and oil in skillet until you can smell garlic; remove garlic with slotted spoon and discard. Add pork and stir-fry quickly for about 3 minutes. Remove from heat and keep warm (Note: 140° oven will keep food warm without further cooking). In a saucepan heat soy sauce, vinegar, sugar and juices from pineapples and pickles. Mix remaining 2 teaspoons of cornstarch with 2 teaspoons of water and stir into juices in saucepan. Cook, stirring constantly, until thickened. Add pineapple, pickles, tomatoes and pepper wedges. Cook for a few seconds longer. Place pork on platter and pour sauce over it. Serve over steamed rice. Makes 4 servings.

PEKING KITCHEN — Stall #508

"Olvera St."
Chunky Lamb

Lamb goes South of the Border with spicy accents, courtesy of the gift emporium named The Latin Shop.

2 lbs lamb
¼ cup olive oil
1 large onion, chopped
1 28-oz can tomatoes
½ cup red wine (optional)
½ tsp oregano, crushed
salt and pepper to taste
2 lbs string beans, washed
½ lb fresh mushrooms, sliced

Cut lamb in bite-size pieces and saute in oil until brown. Add tomatoes, wine, oregano, salt and pepper and cook covered until meat is tender. Break string beans in half or thirds and add to meat with mushrooms and continue cooking until beans are tender. Makes 6 servings.

LATIN SHOP — Stall #150-28

Veal Florentine

Patsy's Pizza knows more about Italian cooking than just making pizzas — here's his gourmet veal recipe.

**16 slices veal,
    pounded thin
4 tbs flour
4-6 tbs butter or
    margarine
6 oz Madeira wine
1 lb fresh spinach,
    washed
2 oz Parmesan
    cheese, grated
⅛ lb proscuitto ham,
    sliced very thin
¼ lb mozzarella
    cheese, sliced
    thin**

Heat oven to 400°.
Place veal between 2 sheets of greaseproof paper and pound flat. Pass veal through flour and saute in 2 tbs butter for 2 minutes. Turn veal and saute for 2 minutes more. Add Maderia wine and cook 1 minute. Remove pan from heat. In a large skillet, saute spinach in 2 tablespoons butter. Place veal in ovenproof casserole with drippings. Place spinach on top of each veal slice and sprinkle with Parmesan cheese. Cover with ham and mozzarella cheese and place in oven for 3 minutes or until thoroughly heated and cheese is melted. Makes 4 servings.

PATSY'S PIZZA — Stall #448

Pulgagi
(Korean beef)

Petite Girl promises that this entree from Korea will not add to your waistline.

**½ onion, thinly
    sliced
1 fresh green onion,
    chopped fine
1 carrot, chopped
    fine
2 cloves garlic,
    crushed
6 tbs soy sauce
1 tsp sugar
½ tsp salt
½ tsp pepper
1 tbs red wine
2 tsp sesame seeds,
    toasted
1½ lbs round
    steak, thinly
    sliced**

Mix together all ingredients except beef and blend thoroughly. Place beef in baking dish and pour sauce mixture over it, making sure each piece of meat is coated. Allow to marinate several hours or overnight in refrigerator. Barbecue meat or put under broiler for 2 to 3 minutes on each side. Garnish meat with additional sesame seeds. Serve with steamed rice. Makes 4 servings.

PETITE GIRL — Stall #150-3

Polynesian Spareribs

Oriental Sportswear at Polynesian Casuals inspired this dish.

3 lbs spareribs, cut into individual ribs
1/3 cup soy sauce
¼ cup granulated sugar
¼ cup brown sugar
1/3 cup pineapple juice
¼ tsp garlic powder
1½ tsp ground ginger
¼ cup ketchup

Heat oven to 400°.
Brown spareribs on both sides and remove fat from pan. Reduce oven heat to 350°. Combine remaining ingredients in a sauce pan and heat thoroughly. Coat each rib with sauce and bake in middle of oven, basting regularly, for one hour. Serve with plain rice or rice with currants or chopped raisins added. Makes 4 servings.

POLYNESIAN CASUALS — Stall #140-Q

Scene Stealers Ham Loaf

A wide selection of prime meats insures Marconda's reputation as butchers par excellance.

1½ lbs ground fresh pork
1½ lbs ground uncooked ham
2 eggs, slightly beaten
3 cups fresh bread crumbs
¼ cup brown sugar
1¼ cups buttermilk
3 tbs prepared horseradish
½ cup orange marmalade

Heat oven to 350°.
Mix pork, ham, eggs, bread crumbs, brown sugar, buttermilk, and horseradish. Press mixture firmly into 2-quart buttered baking dish. Bake for 1½ hours. Loosen sides and invert onto buttered ovenproof platter. Spread top of loaf with orange marmalade. Place back in oven until top is bubbly or broil 3 to 4 inches from heat.
May be baked ahead, turned out, glazed, refrigerated and reheated at party time. Makes 6-8 servings.

MARCONDA'S QUALITY MEATS
Stall #512

DESSERTS

Swedish Krum Kaka

Sweden's finest imports find their way to the Sweden Shop, including this cookie recipe.

1 cup sour cream
¼ cup sugar
1 egg, beaten
2 drops lemon
extract
1 cup flour
2 tbs butter, melted

Whip the sour cream until stiff. Add separately and stir after each addition sugar, egg, lemon extract and flour. Brush Krum Kaka iron with butter and heat. Put a spoonful of batter in center of iron and turn during cooking so that cookies will brown evenly. Roll cookies over a wooden stick or spoon immediately on removing from iron or shape into a cone. Cool on rack. Yield: 50 Cookies.

Optional
Filling for cones:
½ pt heavy cream
2 tbs confectioner's
sugar
vanilla, instant
coffee or cocoa
for flavoring

Whip cream until almost stiff and add sugar. Continue beating and add flavoring and beat until very stiff. Fill each cone with cream just before serving to insure crispness.

SWEDEN SHOP — Stall #150-21

Magical Marzipan Rings

Magic Nut Shop pulls this great recipe out of its bag of tricks with nuts.

1½ lbs almonds,
blanched
1¼ lbs confectioners
sugar
2 egg whites,
unbeaten
1 tsp almond extract

Heat oven to 325°.
Grind almonds until very fine. Mix with sugar, egg whites and almond extract and knead to stiff paste. Wet hands and roll paste on board which is sprinkled with confectioner's sugar. Roll into long piece and cut diagonally into 1" pieces and roll into rings or crescents. Bake on floured cookie sheet about 10 minutes. (Note: over baking causes dryness.) Allow to cool. Makes 4 dozen.

MAGIC NUT SHOP — Stall #522

Best Brownies Yet!

Ralph's Key Shop opens the way to many compliments with these tasty brownies.

1 cup butter or
   margarine
4 squares
   unsweetened
   chocolate
4 eggs
2 cups granulated
   sugar
1 cup flour
   (cake flour is
   preferred)
1 tsp baking powder
1 tsp vanilla
1 cup walnuts,
   chopped

Heat oven to 350°.
Melt butter and chocolate over a double boiler or watch closely if on stove top. Remove from heat and stir to cool. Add each egg separately, mixing well after each addition. Add sugar and mix well. Combine flour and baking powder and add to chocolate mixture. Add vanilla and nuts. Pour batter into well greased and floured large baking pan. Bake for 20 minutes. Cool on a rack, dust with powdered sugar and cut into squares. Yield: 35-40 squares.

RALPH'S KEY SHOP — Stall #552

Fudge Sundae Pie

This Sundae edition at Phil Pearson's Alley Newsstand is a real headliner.

1 3⅝-oz pkg
   chocolate
   pudding mix
1 cup milk
1 cup half-and-half
1 cup heavy
   cream, whipped

1½ pts ice cream
   (flavor of your
   choice)
1 9" pie shell,
   baked and cooled

In a saucepan cook chocolate pudding, milk and half-and-half. Cool. Fold whipped cream into pudding. Drop dollops of ice cream on baked pie crust and pour pudding mixture over ice cream. Freeze until solid and then cover with foil. Remove from freezer 20 minutes before serving. Decorate with additional whipping cream put through a pastry tube and sprinkle with crushed almonds.

Nut Pie Crust:
2 cups flour
1 cup shortening
1 tsp salt
¾ tsp vinegar

1 egg, beaten
3 tbs cold water
¾ cup nuts,
   chopped

Combine flour, shortening and salt and cut into small pebble-size pieces with pastry knife or fork. Add remaining ingredients and mix together until well blended. With hands, press into large ball. Press into 9" pie pan. Prick with fork. Can be refrigerated until needed. Heat oven to 350°.

PHIL PEARSON'S ALLEY NEWSSTAND
Stall #150-1

Baba au Rhum

Try something special on your guests with this rum-flavored treat from those dessert wizards at Michael's Gourmet Pastries.

¼ cup milk, scalded
¼ cup butter
1 pkg yeast
¼ cup orange juice, room temperature
2 egg yolks
¼ cup granulated sugar
1 egg
1 tbs orange rind, grated
1¾ cups flour, sifted
hot rum syrup
whipped cream

Scald milk, add butter and blend. Cool to luke-warm. Sprinkle in yeast and stir until dissolved. In a separate bowl, beat egg yolks and gradually add sugar. Vigorously beat in the whole egg and add milk mixture, orange juice and orange rind. Stir in flour and beat until smooth. Cover batter with a towel and let rise in a warm place until doubled in bulk, about one hour. Stir down batter and spoon into six individual well-greased baba molds or small custard cups, filling them 2/3 full. Let rise, uncovered, until batter reaches the top of the molds, about 30 minutes.
Heat oven to 350°.
Bake 20 minutes or until toothpick comes out clean. Remove from molds and cool on a rack. Place cooled babas on serving platter and marinate with hot rum syrup several hours before serving. Fill each baba with a generous amount of whipped cream.

Hot rum syrup:
1 cup water
1 cup granulated sugar
3 slices orange
2 sticks cinnamon
½ cup rum

Combine all ingredients in a saucepan except the rum and bring to a boil, stirring until sugar is dissolved. Simmer for 5 minutes. Strain and add rum. Yield: 1½ cups.

Whipped cream:
1 cup heavy cream
1 tbs confectioner's sugar
1 tbs rum

Whip cream until almost stiff. Add sugar and rum and continue beating until stiff.

MICHAEL'S GOURMET PASTRIES — #618

Terrific Trifle

Littlejohn's Candies, one of the Market's sweet tooth specialists, reveals the secrets of an old English treat.

- **1 12-oz package prepared cake mix (sponge or pound)**
- **4 tbs raspberry or currant jam**
- **1 2¼-oz package sliced almonds (not the slivered type)**
- **1 cup sweet or medium sherry**
- **¼ cup brandy**
- **1 cup whipping cream**
- **1 tbs fine granulated sugar**
- **1 4-oz package raspberry gelatin**

- **2 cups raspberries (or other berries or fruit, but not fresh pineapple) or 2 10-oz packages frozen berries, well drained**
- **1½ cups boiling water**
- **1 soft custard sauce**
- **¼ lb English toffee, ground up**
- **cherries, berries or other garnish**

Prepare cake mix according to directions on package. Make a day in advance of assembly. Line a glass serving dish or pyrex loaf pan with any type of cake (not too sweet) in about 1" thick slices. Spread jam or jelly over these. Cut the rest of the cake into small cubes and spread over the sliced cake. Sprinkle the almonds throughout, then pour the sherry and brandy over this mixture. Allow it to steep at room temperature for at least 30 minutes. While this mixture is steeping, prepare custard sauce and cool. Also, prepare gelatin with hot water and allow it to cool, but not to set. Chill a mixing bowl in preparation for whipping cream. When the mixture has steeped thoroughly, place berries or fruit on top and pour in cooled gelatin. Place in refrigerator to set. When firm, pour cooled custard over this. Whip the cream, adding sugar when it becomes slightly thickened, then continue whipping until it is stiff. Spread the whipped cream on top of the custard. Garnish with ground-up English toffee and cherries.

Soft Custard Sauce:
- **2 cups milk**
- **3 eggs, slightly beaten**
- **1/3 cup sugar**
- **¼ tsp salt**
- **1 tsp vanilla**

Place 1¾ cups of milk in top of double boiler. Bring to boiling point over direct heat, then place over the boiling water in bottom of the double boiler. Combine eggs, sugar, salt and the remaining milk. Add to scalded milk, stirring constantly. Cook, still stirring constantly, until a coating forms on a spoon. Cool. Add vanilla.

Many variations of this recipe are used in English homes. Each family has its own way to use up odd pieces of cake and fruit. Some soak the cake in orange juice instead of sherry. Some use only whipped gelatin instead of whipped cream and pour custard over the top. Some omit the gelatin entirely, using only whipped cream.

LITTLEJOHN'S CANDIES — Stall #432

"Make Believe" Fruitcake

When your sweet tooth sends out signals follow the advice of Langston's Sausage & Coffee Corner when it suggests this holiday dessert.

1 cup candied
   pineapple
1 cup dates,
   chopped
2 cups walnuts,
   chopped in large
   pieces
1 cup whole
   maraschino
   cherries, drained
¾ cup granulated
   sugar
¾ cup flour
1 tsp baking powder
1 tsp salt
3 eggs, beaten
1 tsp vanilla

Heat oven to 325°.
Mix together pineapple, dates, walnuts and cherries. Sift together sugar, flour, baking powder and salt and then pour over fruit. Beat together eggs and vanilla and pour over mixture. With a wooden spoon, mix gently but well and press into greased 2-lb loaf pan. Bake for 1½ hours. Remove from oven and let stand 15 minutes before removing from pan. Makes 8 servings.

**LANGSTON'S SAUSAGE &
COFFEE CORNER — Stalls #318 & 542**

"Tinsel Town" Date-Nut Bars

Youngsters of all ages will enjoy these snacks as much as they'll delight in the toys, dolls and games at Kip's Toyland.

1 cup dates, cut fine
1 cup walnuts,
   chopped fine
1¼ cups flour
5 tbs sour milk

½ tsp baking
   powder
1 cup brown sugar,
   packed
2 eggs, beaten
pinch of salt

Heat oven to 350°.
Combine all ingredients and mix thoroughly. Pour into a greased 8 x 8 or 7½ x 12 hallow pan and bake 20-25 minutes. Cool and cut into bars.

KIP'S TOYLAND — Stall #150-2

Filmy Dessert Crepes

Michael's Cheesecake suggests — for best results — fill these crepes with fresh fruit or preserves.

1 cup cold water
1¾ cups flour
1 cup milk
4 egg yolks
1 tbs granulated
   sugar
3 tbs cognac
5 tbs butter,
   melted

Using a wooden spoon, combine water and flour and blend until very smooth. Add milk and continue blending thoroughly. Add egg yolks, sugar and cognac, stirring constantly. Add butter and stir well. (Note: should you prefer to use an electric blender, combine all ingredients in blender and whirl for 1½ minutes, or until completely blended.)
Cook crepes in traditional crepe pan or in 8" skillet. Lightly grease pan and pour a heaping tablespoon of batter onto heated pan. Rotate pan to spread evenly. Pour back into bowl any excess. When crepe begins to leave the side of the pan, turn over and cook 2 minutes more. Drop out of pan on wooden board. Yield: 18 crepes.
Can be filled with preserves, fresh fruit and whipped cream, ice cream and topped with chocolate sauce.

MICHAEL'S CHEESECAKE — Stall #434

Pecan Pie "Pacifica"

Here's the Cadillac of pies from the files of Le Mart Dessert Shop, creators of fine pies, tarts and eclairs.

3 eggs
½ cup granulated
   sugar
1 tsp vanilla
1 cup dark Karo
   syrup
½ tsp salt
1 tbs butter
1 cup pecans

Heat oven to 325°.
Beat eggs slightly. Add sugar, vanilla, syrup, salt, butter and nuts. Stir well. Pour into an unbaked 8" pie crust and bake for 50 minutes. (Note: pecans will float to top and form crunchy topping.) Makes 6-8 servings.

Pie Crust:
2 cups pastry flour
½ tsp granulated
   sugar
¼ tsp salt
10 tbs solid
   vegetable
   shortening
5 tbs cold water

Mix flour, sugar, salt and shortening until crumbly. Add water, a little at a time. Form into ball. Place on floured board and roll out. Place in 8" pie tin, gently pressing to fit contours of tin. (Note: overworking of dough will cause toughness.) Makes 2 pie shells. (Note: cover extra pie shell with plastic wrap and freeze.)

LE MART DESSERT SHOP — Stall #530

"Hollywood" Delight Apricot Bars

These fruity dessert bars are recommended by Hanson's Gallery, a shopful of fine burl wood furniture accessories.

1¾ cups oatmeal
1½ cups flour, sifted
1 tsp baking soda
1 cup brown sugar,
   packed
1 cup butter, melted
1 cup walnuts,
   chopped

Heat oven to 350°.
Combine all ingredients and mix well. Press 2/3 of mixture into 8" x 8" ungreased pan. Spread apricot filling evenly over oatmeal mixture and top with remaining oatmeal mixture. Bake for 35 to 40 minutes. Cut into squares when warm but not hot from oven.

Apricot Filling:
½ lb dried apricots
½ cup water
1 cup granulated
   sugar
1 tsp vanilla

Stew apricots in water until soft. Add sugar while apricots are still hot. Remove from heat and cool. Add vanilla.

HANSON GALLERY — Stall #710

Neopolitan Baked Alaska

Good old-fashioned ice cream, like the kind you'll find at Gill's Ice Cream, will make this dessert a real success.

6 egg whites
6 tbs confectioner's
   sugar
¼ tsp vanilla
2 qts neapolitan
   ice cream (vanilla,
   chocolate, straw-
   berry)
sponge cake mix

Make a meringue by beating egg whites until stiff, gradually adding sugar while beating. Add vanilla. Prepare sponge cake according to directions on the package, baking it in a square pan. Cut cake into 2 layers and place side-by-side on board covered with white paper. Put ice cream on cake with ¼" edge of cake uncovered. Cover ice cream and cake with meringue. Place board on cookie sheet and put under broiler 4" below heat and brown meringue quickly. Serve immediately. Makes 8 servings.

GILL'S ICE CREAM — Stall #416

Ticker-Tape Chocolate Cheesecake

Your stock as a gourmet cook will soar with this chocolate cheesecake from E.F. Hutton & Co., members of the New York Stock Exchange.

18 chocolate wafers	1½ lbs cream
¼ cup butter or	cheese, softened
margarine, melted	1 cup granulated
¼ tsp cinnamon	sugar
1 pkg (8 oz) semi-	3 eggs
sweet chocolate	2 tsp cocoa
(or chocolate	1 tsp vanilla
chips)	2 cups sour cream

Heat oven to 350°.
Crush enough wafers to make 1 cup of crumbs. Melt butter in sauce pan. Mix in crumbs and cinnamon. Press crumb mixture on bottom of 9" spring-form pan. Chill. Melt chocolate in top of double boiler. In a large bowl, beat the cream cheese until fluffy and smooth, using electric mixer. Beat in sugar. Add eggs, one at a time. Add melted chocolate, cocoa and vanilla, blending thoroughly. Beat in sour cream. Pour into spring-form pan. Bake 1 hour and 10 minutes. Cool at room temperature, then chill in refrigerator overnight. (Note: cake will still by runny, but becomes firm when chilled.) Makes 8-10 servings.

E.F. HUTTON & COMPANY

Gadabout Coffee Cake

Need energy for globe-trotting? Farmers Market Travel & Tours suggest launching your next trip with their bon voyage cake.

¼ lb butter	1 tsp salt
½ cup solid vegetable shortening	1 13-oz can evaporated milk
2 cups sugar	1 tsp vanilla
3 eggs, beaten	1 cup nuts, chopped
3¼ cups flour, sifted	2 tsp cinnamon
4 tsp baking powder	1/3 cup sugar

Heat oven to 350°.
Cream together butter, vegetable shortening, sugar and eggs. Sift flour, baking powder and salt together. Add alternately with evaporated milk to creamed mixture. Add vanilla. Fold nuts in by hand. Grease and flour angel food pan. Put small amount of batter into bottom of pan, sprinkle with cinnamon and 1/3 cup sugar mixed together and repeat until all ingredients are used. Bake 70 minutes or until toothpick comes out clean. Makes 10 servings.

FARMERS MARKET TRAVEL & TOURS
Stall #1024

"Sunset Strip" Apple Coffee Cake

From the breakfast specialists at Bob's Coffee & Doughnuts is the secret behind preparing this round-the-clock favorite.

½ cup butter
1 cup granulated sugar
1 cup sour cream
2 eggs
2 cups flour
1 tsp baking soda
1 tsp baking powder
½ tsp salt
1 tsp vanilla

Cream butter until soft. Add sugar and ½ cup sour cream. Beat until light and fluffy. Add eggs, one at a time, beating well after each addition. Sift dry ingredients together and add to creamed mixture, alternating with remaining sour cream and mix thoroughly. Stir in vanilla. Pour half the batter into a well greased tube pan.

Filling:
- **¼ cup granulated sugar**
- **1/3 cup brown sugar**
- **1 tsp cinnamon**
- **¼ cup walnuts, chopped fine**
- **1 large green apple, peeled, cored and sliced thin**

Heat oven to 350°.
Combine all ingredients except apples and mix well. Place all apple slices on batter in pan. Sprinkle half of the sugar mixture over apples. Pour remaining batter into pan and spinkle top with sugar mixture. Bake 45 minutes or until toothpick comes out of cake clean. Cool and unmold, right side up. Makes 12 servings.

BOB'S COFFEE AND DOUGHNUTS
Stall #450

Ice Cream a la Mini-Mousse

This mini-mousse, courtesy of the recipe files of Bennett's Ice Cream, will make a sweet hit with young and old alike.

- **8 oz semi-sweet chocolate squares**
- **½ cup granulated sugar**
- **¼ cup water or coffee**
- **5 egg yolks**
- **1 tsp vanilla**
- **5 egg whites, stiffly beaten**
- **1 qt coffee ice cream**
- **2 oz almonds, grated or chopped fine**

Melt together chocolate, sugar and water, stirring occasionally to avoid sticking. Remove from heat, place pan in cold water and stir until cool. When cool, add one egg yolk at a time, mixing thoroughly as each yolk is added. Add vanilla. Fold in egg whites and set aside. Line a mold with coffee ice cream, leaving a well in the middle. Fill well with chocolate mixture and freeze. Unmold on serving platter and top with nuts. Makes 8-10 servings.

BENNETT'S ICE CREAM — Stall #548

"Tarzana" Oatmeal Cake

Barbara's Cravats, an import shop featuring accessories for men, selects a cake with a masculine touch of class.

1½ cups boiling water	1 cup walnuts, chopped medium
¼ lb margarine, melted	1½ cups flour, sifted
1 cup quick oatmeal	½ tsp salt
1 cup brown sugar, packed	½ tsp baking powder
1 cup granulated white sugar	1 tsp cinnamon
2 eggs, beaten	1 tsp baking soda

Heat oven to 350°.
Pour water and margarine over oatmeal and let stand 20 minutes. Add brown sugar, eggs and nuts. Sift together remaining ingredients and add to oatmeal mixture, blending thoroughly. Pour into a well-greased 9" square pan and bake for 45 minutes. Cool 5 minutes and spread with topping.

Topping:

7 tsp evaporated milk	½ cup walnuts or almonds, chopped
1 cup brown sugar, packed	¾ cup coconut, shredded

Mix together all the above ingredients and spread on cake. Place under broiler about 3 minutes or until coconut is toasted.

**BARBARA'S CRAVATS
Stall #150-10**

"Huntington Hartford" Hobo Toast

New styles are the Balcony Beauty Shop's business, and they've created a clever cookie recipe for "hobo" appetites.

½ cup brown sugar	2 tbs baking powder
½ cup white sugar	1 cup dates, chopped
3 eggs, beaten	
10 graham crackers, crushed fine	1 cup walnuts, chopped

Heat oven to 350°.
Combine all ingredients and mix well. Pour into well-greased 13"x9"x2" pan and bake for 35 minutes. Cut into squares. Cool and serve.

BALCONY BEAUTY SHOP — Stall #850½

Precious Gem Cookies

Add sparkle to a meal with these gems from Walter Wright's Jewelry.

2 egg whites
pinch of salt
2/3 cup sugar
1 tsp vanilla
1 cup
  chocolate bits
1 cup pecans,
  chopped

Heat oven to 350°.
Beat egg whites and salt until foamy. Add sugar gradually and beat until stiff. Add remainder of the ingredients. Cover cookie sheet with foil. Drop cookies by the teaspoon. Place in oven on middle rack. Turn off heat and leave in oven overnight. Remove from foil with spatula.

WALTER WRIGHT — Stall #150-20

Crunchy Peach Romanoff

From Carson's Candy Kitchens, where you can actually watch sweets being made, is this compliment-catching recipe featuring fresh peaches.

4 egg yolks
1 scant cup
  granulated sugar
1 cup sherry
1 cup heavy cream,
  whipped stiff
4 fresh peaches,
  sliced
¼ lb praline,
  chopped

Beat egg yolks, add sugar and mix well. Add sherry and cook in double boiler 5 minutes, stirring constantly. Remove from heat and cool. When cold, fold in cream. Spoon mixture over individual servings of peach slices. Sprinkle praline over top of each serving. Makes 8 servings.

CARSON'S CANDY KITCHENS
Stalls #212-426-526

"San Fernando" Strawberry Pie

The fresh strawberries at Kludjian and Stone Tropical Fruits stand are begging to star in this delectable dessert.

**2 baskets fresh
    strawberries,
    washed and
    stems removed
1 4-oz pkg cream
    cheese, softened
1 7-oz jar marsh-
    mallow whip
1 9" pie crust,
    baked and cooled
1 8-oz jar currant
    jelly
1 tsp lemon juice**

Slice half of the strawberries in a bowl and set aside. Combine cream cheese and marshmallow whip and blend until creamy and smooth. Spread cream cheese mixture evenly on bottom of pie crust. Place sliced strawberries on cream cheese, making sure no cream cheese shows through. Arrange the whole strawberries near the edge of the crust, side by side with points (tips) up. Place the remaining whole berries in the center, points up, in an attractive design. Heat jelly and lemon juice in a saucepan until melted, stirring constantly. Remove from heat. Stir to cool. When cool, spoon over berries making sure the entire surface is covered and each berry is coated. Chill at least 3 hours. Makes 6 servings.

Pastry Shell:
**1 cup flour
½ tsp salt
1/3 cup butter or
    solid vegetable
    shortening
¼ cup orange juice,
    chilled**

Heat oven to 375°.
Add salt to flour and cut shortening into it with pastry cutter or fork. When mixture is consistency of little pebbles, add chilled orange juice and continue cutting. Make dough into a ball and roll out on floured board. Run spatula under dough to loosen from board. Lift dough and gently place into 9" pie pan. Prick dough with fork and bake 10-12 minutes or until lightly golden brown. Remove from oven and place on rack to cool.

**KLUDJIAN & STONE TROPICAL FRUITS
Stall #324**

Mexican Pan Pudding Ole

Castillo's Spanish Kitchen, a little bit of Old Mexico right here in Farmers Market, is where this recipe originates.

1 qt water
1 lb brown sugar
1 3-inch stick cinnamon
4 cloves
6 slices white bread, crust removed and cubed
3 apples, peeled, cored and sliced
1 cup raisins
1 cup peanuts, chopped
½ cup blanched almonds
½ cup medium cheddar cheese, cubed

Heat oven to 350°.
Combine water, sugar, cinnamon and cloves and boil until syrupy. Grease a casserole and cover bottom with a layer of bread cubes; then add a layer of apples, raisins, peanuts, almonds and cheese. Repeat layering until all ingredients have been used. Remove cinnamon stick and cloves from syrup and pour over apple mixture. Bake for 30 minutes. Serve hot. Makes 8-10 servings.

CASTILLO'S SPANISH KITCHEN
Stall # 510- 322

After-Theatre Cafe Brulot

Connoisseurs love the selection of coffees from all over the world at Mr. K's Gourmet Food & Coffee.

4 oz cognac
2 small cinnamon sticks
8 whole cloves
10 pieces of lump sugar
2 tbs chocolate syrup
2 long strips orange peel
2 strips lemon peel
2 cups demitasse- strength coffee

Place all ingredients except hot demitasse coffee in chafing dish. Ignite cognac with match and stir ingredients until well blended. After a minute or two, slowly pour in the hot black coffee and continue to stir. (In winter, heat cognac before using.) To serve, strain into Brulot or demitasse cups. Makes 4 servings.

MR. K'S GOURMET FOOD & COFFEE
Stall #430

Honey Walnut Slices

Walnuts, plus every variety of nut you've ever heard of, is for sale at Magic Nut Too.

1 cup oil	**4 cups flour**
2 cups water	**1 tsp baking soda**
1 cup honey	**1 tsp baking powder**
1 cup granulated sugar	**4 oz almonds, blanched, whole or halved**
1½ tsp cinnamon	
1 tsp salt	
2 cups walnuts, finely chopped	

Heat oven to 350°.
In a large sauce pan, mix oil, water, honey, sugar, cinnamon and salt. Bring to a boil and add walnuts. Mix thoroughly. Remove from heat. Combine flour, baking soda and baking powder and stir into mixture until all flour is absorbed and blended. Pour into a greased 9" x 13" pan, spreading evenly. Score cake into slices about 1½" x 3". Press an almond in each slice and bake 40-45 minutes. Cool 10 minutes then pour syrup over warm cake and allow to stand 24 hours. Yield: 48 pieces

Syrup:

3 cups granulated sugar	**1 cup water**
	juice of one lemon

Bring sugar and water to a boil, cooking over low heat until you can form a small ball when small amount of mixture is dropped in cold water (approximately 10 minutes). Cool and add lemon juice.

MAGIC NUT, TOO! — Stall #234

Crunchy Pecan Pumpkin Pie

Pecans add punch to holiday pumpkin pie, as suggested by World Religious Arts.

1 cup fresh pumpkin, steamed and mashed or 1 cup canned pumpkin	**½ tsp nutmeg**
	½ cup finely chopped pecans
1 cup maple syrup	**3 eggs, well beaten**
½ tsp ginger	**2 cups heavy cream**
1 tsp cinnamon	**½ tsp salt**

Heat oven to 450°.
Mix all ingredients together. Pour into an unbaked pastry shell and bake in hot oven for 10 minutes. Then reduce heat to moderate (350°) and bake for at least 20 to 25 minutes more or until knife comes out clean when inserted in center of pie. Cool before serving.

Pastry Shell:

1½ cups all purpose flour	**½ cup shortening**
½ tsp salt	**2 to 3 tbs ice water**

Add salt to flour and cut shortening into it with pastry cutter or forks. When mixture is consistency of little pebbles add ice water and continue cutting. Make dough into a ball and roll out on floured bread. Run spatula under dough to loosen from board. Lift dough and gently place into 9" pie pan.

WORLD RELIGIOUS ARTS — Stall #140-D

Treats with Jams & Jellies

Mr. K.'s Jams & Jellies are prized by all and he has learned many ways to use them.

A SIMPLE GLAZE FOR CHICKEN:

1 4-oz jar plum jam
¼ cup soy sauce
1 tsp lemon juice
½ tsp onion flakes
  or powder
¼ tsp dry mustard

Heat oven to 350°.
Combine all ingredients in a sauce pan and bring to a boil. Spoon over chicken parts arranged in a glass baking dish. Bake for one hour, basting regularly. Should you need more liquid, add a little warm water.

DRESS UP YOUR DINNER PLATE:

Place a canned peach or pear half, cut side up on a baking dish. Use one piece of fruit per serving. Fill the fruit with a scant spoonful of jam or jelly and place under the broiler until jam begins to bubble. Place fruit on plate and sprinkle with ground nuts.

FOR A QUICK FRUIT PIE GLAZE:

Melt a small (8 oz) jar of currant jelly in a sauce pan and add ½ tsp lemon juice or 1 tsp orange liqueur. Arrange strawberries, boysenberries, etc. in a baked pie shell and spoon on glaze covering each piece of fruit. Chill several hours before serving.

MR. K.'S JAMS & JELLIES — Stall #524

Tricks with Fruit

Here are a trio of crowd-pleasers, made all the more delicous when you use fresh fruit from Meshulam's Citrus and Fruit Packs.

FRESH PINEAPPLE

To select the proper ripeness of a pineapple: color alone does not indicate ripeness; select the right size, then with your finger thump the pineapple as you would a watermelon. A full dull sound indicates a ripe pineapple. It is easy to slice if you stand the pineapple up, holding the green top as a handle. With a sharp knife, cut down on the skin deep enough to cut out the eyes. You are not wasting any of the pineapple as the meat under the skin is not the sweetest. When completely peeled, cut off the bottom of the pineapple. Slice the pineapple into ½" wide slices, still holding the green top as a handle. Serve in full slices or cut the slices in half. Hawaiian pineapples do not have a tough core — it is not necessary to remove. As a dessert, the pineapple can be served in chunks with ½ cup green or white creme de menthe poured over the chunks. Spear a maraschino cherry on each of 12 toothpicks and then stick into pineapple chunks. Sprigs of fresh mint will also add charm to this dish. Makes 8-10 servings.

BROILED GRAPEFRUIT

**1 grapefruit cut
  in half
2 tbs brown sugar
1 tsp butter or
  margarine
maraschino cherry**

Separate the grapefruit segments from the membrane and shell by inserting thin paring knife between them. Sprinkle sugar evenly on grapefruit and dot with butter. Place in baking dish and put under broiler and heat until sugar melts and starts to bubble. Remove from broiler and place on salad plates, pouring any remaining syrup from pan onto grapefruit. Garnish with maraschino cherry. Makes 2 servings.

STRAWBERRIES

**1 basket fresh
  strawberries,
  washed and
  stems left on
½ pt sour cream
½ cup brown sugar,
  packed solid**

Place each ingredient in separate serving bowls. To eat, dip tip of strawberry in sour cream and then brown sugar. Makes 4 servings.

**MESHULAMS CITRUS AND FRUIT PACKS
Stall #612**

Directory

STORES

. . . You can find treasures from the Orient — the silks, clothing, jewelry. Hand-made leather goods from American Indians. Marvelous South Seas wood carvings, tapa cloth, Polynesian clothing. And fine arts and crafts from the world over. You'll also discover a colorful collection of precious stones, shops catering to men, women and children, and thousands of things for both the home and outdoors.

RESTAURANTS

. . . Eat in a foreign language — Chinese, Italian, French, Spanish, Mexican, Cantonese and others offering international delicacies. This plus sea foods, pit barbecues, and delectable desserts. From 26 different kitchens you can select a salad from one, an entree from another, and a beverage and dessert from still others — just about every food imaginable. Then pick out an outdoors table under a cooling umbrella, relax and enjoy the unusual.

MARKET SECTION

. . . There are 10 stalls displaying beautiful morning-fresh vegetables and fruits, 11 meat markets featuring the finest prime beef, lamb, pork, fish and poultry, two cheese shops and fancy groceries stocked with a myriad of imported and domestic gourmet items, and butchers and bakers and candlestick makers.

STALL	TENANT
150	**ALEXANDER'S GROCERY** Complete line of groceries, gourmet foods, frozen foods, health foods
328	**ALTABET'S FLOWER SHOP** Potted plants, cut flowers, arrangements
750	**BARBER SHOP**
850½	**BALCONY BEAUTY SHOP** Hairstyling, manicuring, wig cleaning
	BARENGO VINEYARDS Wine tasting and sales
548	**BENNETT'S ICE CREAM** Fancy ice cream, fountain service, special molds and ice cream cakes for all occasions
126	**BISBANO'S CITRUS** Citrus fruits and fruit gift packs
130	**BISBANO'S PRODUCE** Fresh vegetables and fruits — in and out of season
450	**BOB'S COFFEE & DOUGHNUTS** Coffee, tea, milk, doughnuts

334	**BORIS JUICE AND SALAD BAR** 21 kinds of juices, fruit salads
740	**BRYAN'S PIT BARBECUE** Pit barbecued beef, pork, ham chicken and spare ribs, barbecued beans, sauerkraut
212/426 526	**CARSON'S CANDY KITCHENS** You can watch your candy being made
322/510	**CASTILLO'S SPANISH KITCHEN** Tacos, tamales, enchiladas, rice, beans
826	**CEDRIC'S FLOWER SHOP** Cut flowers, planters, arrangements
744	**CHINESE KITCHEN** Chow mein, chop suey, egg foo young
412	**CHRIS'S COFFEE SHOP** Coffee, waffles, sandwiches, breakfasts
330	**CLARA AND JOE'S BREAD BIN** Over 110 varieties of bread & rolls
318/542	**COFFEE CORNER** Coffee, tea, milk, sweet rolls
1020	**CORAL REEF BIRD SHOP** Birds of all kinds, hamsters, turtles, cages, pet foods and supplies
920	**CORAL REEF GIFT SHOP** South Seas Island imports, baskets, jewelry
922	**CRYSTAL DREAMS** Exclusive designs in cut crystal and monograms. Custom made at the shop
	B. DALTON, PICKWICK BOOKSTORE Hardcover & paperback books

110	**DU-PAR'S BAKERY** 25 different varieties of home-made pies
210	**DU-PAR'S RESTAURANT** Inside dining—famous for their pies. Excellent service, 6:30 a.m. till 1:30 a.m.
222	**EGG BASKET** Eggs at their freshest
	FARMERS MARKET AUTOMOTIVE Mechanic on duty daily
236	**FARMER'S MARKET CHEESE SHOP** 200 varieties of imported and domestic cheeses, cold meats and smoked fish
144	**FARMER'S MARKET FRUIT AND PRODUCE** Wonderful produce—in and out of season
550	**FARMERS MARKET NEWSSTAND** Newspapers, magazines and paper backs
114	**FARMERS MARKET PORK SHOP** Fine Eastern pork products exclusively—country style & link sausage
712	**FARMERS MARKET SHOE REPAIR** Shoes and handbag repairing
1024	**FARMERS MARKET TRAVEL & TOURS** Travel Agency
616	**FARMERS MARKET VARIETY STORE** Notions, games, jewelry, souvenirs, stationery

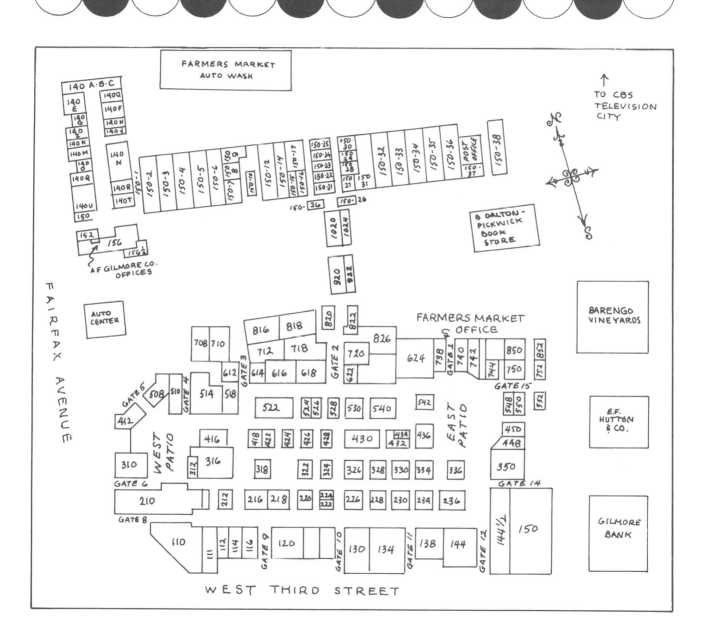

234 MAGIC NUT, TOO
Dried and glazed fruits, nuts,
fruit packs

718 MAGLIANO JEWELRY SHOP
Fine and costume jewelry, watches

512/514 MARCONDA'S QUALITY MEATS
Meats cut to order. Also chopped
meats, meat loaf and barbecue
specialties

518 MESHULAM'S BURBANK STALL
Full line of fruits and vegetables

**612 MESHULAM'S CITRUS AND
FRUIT PACKS**
Gift fruit packs—shipped anywhere

424 MESHULAM'S FRUIT FAIR
Fresh fruits—in and out of season

434 MICHAEL'S CHEESECAKE
Cheesecake, continental desserts,
blintzes

618 MICHAEL'S GOURMET PASTRIES
Bread, cakes, cookies and pastry,
coffee cakes and sweet rolls
baked here

**436 MICHAEL'S OCEAN FOODS
OYSTER BAR**
Fish & sea foods, sea food salads

742 MORT'S
Meats, salads and sandwiches

430 MR. K'S GOURMET FOOD & COFFEE
16 different bulk coffees, 18 different bulk teas & 50 packaged
varieties, spices

312 OLD ENGLISH FISH AND CHIPS
Fish, salads and Friday-burgers

448 PATSY'S PIZZA
A variety of Italian foods, including
pizza

508 PEKING KITCHEN
Chinese food

540 PHIL'S ROUNDUP
Salads, hot dogs, hamburgers,
sandwiches, stuffed cabbage and
other hot plates

818 PITTS GARDEN SHOP
Plants, shrubs and garden
accessories

226 PURITAN POULTRY
Fresh poultry and game birds

552 RALPH'S KEY SHOP
Makes keys, sharpens knives and
scissors

622 THE REFRESHER
Soft drinks

**216 ROGER'S FARMERS MARKET
POULTRY**
Fresh poultry and game birds

230 ST MORITZ BAKERY
Continental pastries

18 SAUNDERS POULTRY
Fresh poultry and game birds

**752 SHOE SHINE AND PLASTIC
LAMINATION**

820/822 TAXCO SHOP
Mexican imports, baskets and
jewelry

310 TONY'S PIZZA SPAGHETTI
Also lasagna, meat balls, mine-
strone, eggplant Parmesan
mostaccioli, baked eggplant, veal
cutlet and ravioli

350 TUSQUELLAS MEAT
The finest in quality meats—
famous for Tusquellas supreme
ham and bacon

138 **TUSQUELLAS SEAFOODS**
All kinds of fresh and frozen fish
122 **VEGETABLE HAVEN**
Fruits, vegetables, herbs
336 **VINCENT'S FINE FOODS**
Short ribs, beef, ham and Italian specialties
738 **YOLANDA'S ITALIAN KITCHEN**
Spaghetti, ravioli, chicken and meat balls

STORE SECTION

140-G, H **AMALIA'S HANDBAGS**
Handbags and accessories
150-8 **ARTS AND CRAFTS BY VANITY STUDIOS**
Artists' materials & craft supplies
150-10 **BARBARA'S CRAVATS**
Men's neckwear, hosiery, belts, shirts, handkerchiefs—imported and domestic
140-E **BRUCE WILLIAMS WESTERN FRONTIER SHOP #2**
Western & Indian wear, boots, moccasins
152 **BRUSH SHOP**
A thousand different kinds of brushes and another thousand related items
150-15 **BUTTONS AND BOWS**
Buttons, Japanese & Israeli imports
140-T **CAMERA EXCHANGE**
All makes of cameras and camera accessories, films, developing and printing
150-32 **CAMPBELL'S MEN'S SHOP**
Men's sportswear & accessories

150-31 **CANDLES BY DREW**
Candles and accessories
150 **GEORGE CHANN**
Portraits & hand painted ceramics
150-14 **CHILDREN'S WORLD**
Apparel for infants and children
150-25 **CHUCK'S**
Sandwiches & special dish ea. day
150-33 **DOROTHE—MATERNITY FASHIONS**
150-30 **FAR EAST TRADERS**
Imports from the Orient
120 **FARMERS MARKET AUTO WASH**
150-34 **FARMERS MARKET BEAUTY SALON**
Complete beauty salon, chiropodist
150-27 **FARMERS MARKET GEM SHOP**
Authentic hand made Indian jewelry
140-R **FARMERS MARKET RECORDS & RADIOS**
Wide selection of records & radios
150-26 **FARMERS MARKET STATIONERY 'N CARDS**
Contemporary and unique personalized stationery and cards
150-36 **FIESTA FOOTWEAR**
Leisure and casual shoes
140-M **FUN SHOP**
Magic and tricks, jokes and favors
160 **A.F. GILMORE COMPANY**
140-K **GLASS BLOWER**
Novelties, different jewelry
156½ **GOLD MINE JEWELERS**
Importers—manufacturers 14 and 18 karat gold jewelry

140-1 INDIAN TRADING POST
Authentic hand made pottery, Navajo rugs, paintings, genuine sterling turquoise jewelry

150-24 INTERNATIONAL SHOP
Gifts from 28 countries, 5 continents

150-16 LORRAINE KAYE
Sportswear

140-0 KIAN'S GALLERY
Metal sculpture

150-35 KING'S CASUALS
Dresses, sportswear, suits—larger sizes

150-2 KIP'S TOYLAND
Fine toys, games and dolls

150-28 LATIN SHOP
Gifts from South America, Spain, Italy

150-29 LITTLE MEXICO MART
Hats, baskets, Mexican tinware and gifts

150-9 LORETTA'S NEEDLEPOINT STUDIO
Patterns, yarns and instructions

140 A, B, C MILLESON'S SPORTING GOODS
Sporting goods, rainwear and hats

156 OLIVER'S PLACE
Gourmet cookware & kitchen & dining accessories

150-38 DAVID ORGELL
Gifts in silver and china—antiques

150-12 PANTS WORLD
Pants & tops for children & adults

150-5 PAPER SHOP
Party supplies, cards & stationery

150-3 PETITE GIRL
Small sizes only

150-1 PHIL'S NEWSSTAND
Magazines, local and out-of-town newspapers, paper backs

140-Q POLYNESIAN CASUALS
Hawaiian and Oriental sportswear

POST OFFICE

150 22, 2 REDWOOD SHOP
Redwood, rare woods, copper and brass

150-4 ROOS LINEN SHOP
Linens, bedding, aprons and handkerchiefs

156 RUG CRAFTERS
Speed-tufting supplies for the home craftsmen

140-J SCRIPTCRAFT JEWELRY
Gold wire pins, bracelets, earrings, tie clips

150-21 SWEDEN SHOP
Scandinavian imports

140-F TIME-LIFE BOOKS
Buy single titles or complete series. Come in and browse

140-N TODAY'S GIRL
Famous brands hosiery—tops and bottoms

150-7 KENNETH TRASK, OPTICIANS
Sun glasses, regular prescriptions filled

150-6 TUNSTALL'S GIFT SHOP
Fine imported and domestic gifts

150-17 WESTERN FRONTIER MOCCASIN & LEATHER SHOP
Western & Indian wear, boots, moccasins

140-D **WORLD RELIGIOUS ARTS**
   Religious articles of all faiths,
   items of spiritual and decorative
   design

150-37 **WRAP AND MAIL SERVICE**
   Gift wrapping and cards

150-20 **WALTER WRIGHT
   CONTEMPORARY JEWELRY**
   Contemporary jewelry and unset
   stones

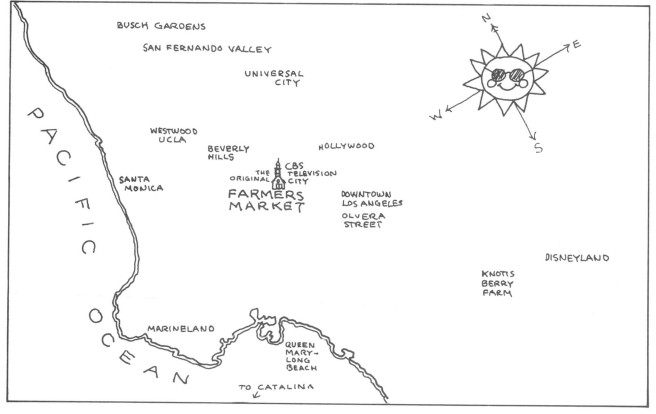

Index

POULTRY

SALADS

SALADS (Continued)

SEAFOOD

SOUPS

VEGETABLES

VEGETABLES (Continued)

The magic of making fresh
peanut butter is unveiled at Magee's.

Apples are in season year-round at this fruit stand.